ACOL BRIDGE MADE EASY

More and more people are finding out what a great joy it is to play bridge. You can learn at any age, but one thing is sure. You will wish you had started earlier.

Bridge is the most stimulating, most intriguing, most fascinating, most challenging of all card games. It will give you more lasting pleasure than any other recreation because of its unending variety. One never tires of bridge.

And yet, bridge is easy . . . easy enough to learn to play a respectable game. *Acol Bridge Made Easy* has been a popular starting point with the first edition running through six impressions. It will have you playing bridge in just a few short hours. Time will pass most quickly and agreeably for you. Once you start playing, you will want to play again and again. Study *Acol Bridge Made Easy* closely and you will have a sound grounding in the game. Happy bridging.

Ron Klinger has represented Australia in many world championship events since 1976 when he won the inaugural Bols Brilliancy Prize. Major successes include the Far East Pairs Championship twice and the South Pacific Teams Championship as well as every significant Australian national title. He has written over thirty books, several of which have been translated into foreign languages. As well as teaching regularly in Australia, he conducts teaching tours in other countries including Great Britain.

ACOL BRIDGE MADE EASY

Ron Klinger

LONDON

VICTOR GOLLANCZ

in association with

PETER CRAWLEY

First published in Great Britain October 1986
in association with Peter Crawley
by Victor Gollancz Ltd
Sixth impression 1994
New edition first published 1997
in association with Peter Crawley
by Victor Gollancz
A imprint of the Cassell Group
Wellington House, 125 Strand, London WC2R 0BB
Reprinted 1998

A catalogue record for this book
is available from the British Library

ISBN 0 575 06359 9

Typeset in Australia by Modern Bridge Publications,
60 Kameruka Road, Northbridge, NSW 2063, Australia
Printed in Great Britain by
St Edmundsbury Press Ltd, Bury St Edmunds, Suffolk

To Keri

Contents

Foreword

Bridge is easily the world's most popular card game. It is played in over a hundred countries and has an estimated following in excess of 60 million players.

The popularity of bridge is surging as increasing leisure enables more and more people to take up worthwhile and stimulating recreations. Bridge is unrivalled when it comes to card games that offer a significant challenge.

Bridge is a social asset and is played by both sexes. It has numerous advantages over other recreations and sports. It can be played under any weather conditions and can be played under the most severe physical handicaps. The deaf can play bridge and so can the blind. A blind bridge player competed in the 1978 World Championships!

Bridge is not an 'old person's game' and children of seven years and younger have been taught to play. More and more young people are taking up bridge, and players in their twenties have won world championships.

On the other hand, age is no barrier to bridge which can be both enjoyed and played successfully at any age. Players in their seventies have won world titles competing against all ages and likewise, players in their eighties have won national championships against all comers. The main complaint of those who do not take up the game early in life is the regret that they did not take it up sooner.

Chapter 1

FROM WHIST TO BRIDGE

A SERIES OF FUN GAMES FOR BEGINNERS

What type of game is bridge?
There are two basic families of card games. In one, the aim is
to form combinations of cards, e.g., Gin Rummy, Canasta,
where the aim is to collect groups such as three nines, four
fives, or runs in the same suit such as 7-8-9 of clubs, Q-J-10-9
of hearts, etc. Contract Bridge belongs to the other in which
the aim is to win *tricks*. Other games in the bridge family are
Whist, Solo, Five Hundred and Euchre.

The form of bridge played today is called Contract Bridge,
which can be played socially (rubber bridge) or competitively
(duplicate bridge). It was devised in 1925, prior to which the
form of bridge played was Auction Bridge which became
popular at the beginning of the 20th century. Bridge itself
developed at the end of the 19th century from the game of
Whist which can be traced back to the 17th century. The word
'bridge' has its ancestry in the Russian word 'Biritch' or
Russian Whist.

Bridge is played by four people, two playing as partners
against the other two. Partners sit opposite each other. You
will need a card table, two packs of cards (though you can
manage with one pack), score pads and pencils.

How many cards are in the pack?

A pack (or deck) of 52 cards is used. There are no jokers. There are four suits: spades ♠, hearts ♡, diamonds ◊ and clubs ♣. Each suit has thirteen cards, the highest being the ace, followed by the king, queen, jack, 10, 9, 8, 7, 6, 5, 4, 3, down to the 2 which is the lowest.

How do we choose partners?

You may agree to play in fixed partnerships, such as husband and wife against the other couple (probably the worst possible arrangement), but unless there is some other agreement, it is usual to draw for partners. This is done by spreading out the pack, face down, and each player picking a card. The two who draw the higher cards play as partners against the other two, normally for one or two 'rubbers'.

After a rubber has been completed, cards are drawn again to form two new partnerships. If, in drawing for partners, two or more cards of the same rank are turned up, then the tie is split according to suit, the suits ranking from the highest, spades, through hearts and diamonds to the lowest, clubs.

For example, A, B, C and D are drawing for partners. The cards turned up are A: ◊8 B: ♠J C: ♠5 D: ♡8. What are the partnerships? *(Answer:* B-D against A-C)

A wit has said that in bridge there is good news and bad news. The good news is that you always have a partner. The bad news is . . . exactly the same.

Who deals?

The person who draws the highest card has the right to choose a seat (the most comfortable one), which pack of cards to use for dealing and also becomes the dealer on the first hand. The next dealer will be the person on the left of the previous dealer and so on in clockwise rotation.

The player on the dealer's left shuffles the cards and puts them face down on his right. ('If you would avoid a fight, place the cards upon your right.') The dealer picks the pack up and passes it to the player on dealer's right to 'cut' (take a number of cards from the top of the pack and place these cards face down next to the remainder). The dealer completes the 'cut' and 'deals' the cards, one at a time, face down, clockwise, starting with the player on the left, until all 52 are dealt.

How many cards will each player have? Who receives the last card? *(Answers:* 13; the dealer)

It is etiquette not to pick up your cards until the deal is complete. This gives everyone equal time and allows a misdeal to be corrected. During the deal, the dealer's partner shuffles the other pack for the next deal. That is why two packs are used, to speed up the game. After being shuffled, the cards are put on the shuffler's right, ready for the next dealer.

In this diagram representing a bridge table and four players, North (N), East (E), South (S) and West (W), the dealer is South.

(a) Who shuffles the pack with which South is going to deal?
(b) Who cuts this pack?
(c) Who receives the first card dealt?
(d) Who is shuffling the other pack while South is dealing?
(e) Where is the other pack placed after it is shuffled?
(f) Who will be the next dealer?

Answers: (a) West (b) East (c) West (d) North (e) On North's right (f) West

The start of play

After picking up your cards, sort them into suits. It is usual to separate the red suits from the blacks and also to put your cards in order of rank in each suit. Each bridge hand has two distinct parts: the bidding (the 'auction') and the play. The bidding starts with the dealer, but more about the bidding later.

It is worthwhile playing a number of games first which do not involve any bidding. These games do illustrate the principles of play and once the ideas involved in the play are understood and absorbed, the objects and rules of the bidding are much easier to understand.

PRE-BRIDGE GAME 1 — NO-TRUMPS WHIST

Each player receives 13 cards. Opposite players are partners. There is no bidding, no dummy and no trump suit. The player on the left of the dealer makes the 'opening lead', that is, places one card face up on the table. Each player in turn in clockwise order plays a card face up. That group of four cards, one from each player, is called a *trick*.

In no-trumps, a trick is won by the highest card of the suit led.

The partnership that wins a trick gathers up the four cards and places them in a neat pile face down. The player who won the trick starts the play to the next trick, i.e., 'leads to the next trick'. Play continues until all 13 tricks have been played and each side then counts up the number of tricks won. The side winning more than six tricks is the winner and is the only side that scores points.

The first card played to a trick is called the 'lead'. Each subsequent player must play a card of the same suit as the lead, if possible. This is known as 'following suit'. The basic law of play is: You *must follow suit if possible.*

If unable to follow suit at no-trumps, you should discard those cards which you judge to be worthless. When it is your turn, you may play a high card or a low card, as you choose, but *you must follow suit if you can.* Even though you could play a high card to win the trick, this might be a foolish move if you can tell partner's card is going to win the trick anyway.

Scoring

We play a **rubber** of bridge. A rubber is **best of three games.** The first side to score **100 points or more** in tricks won scores a **game.** The first side to win two games wins the rubber. A 2-0 win scores 700 bonus points, a 2-1 wins scores 500.

The trick score in NO-TRUMPS is:
30 points for each trick won over six, plus 10.

So, 7 tricks (making 1NT) is worth 40 points, 8 tricks (2NT) is worth 70, 9 tricks (3NT) is worth 100, and so on.

A bridge scoresheet looks like this:

WE	THEY

Trick scores are written below the line, bonus scores above the line. At the end of a game, a line is ruled across both columns. Both sides start the next game from zero. At the end of a rubber the scores in each column are tallied and the higher scoring side is the winner.

The difference between the two scores is rounded to the nearest 100 (e.g., 870 goes to 900, 820 goes to 800; 850 goes down to 800). The score is then entered as the number of 100s won or lost.

For example, if you won by 940, your scoresheet will read '+9' while their scoresheet would record '–9'.

Strategy at no-trumps

Prefer to lead your longest suit and keep on with that suit. When the others run out, your remaining cards in that suit will be winners, since they cannot win the trick if they cannot follow suit. As players lead their own long suit, it is best to return partner's led suit, unless you have a strong suit of your own, and usually avoid returning a suit led by the opposition.

The card to lead: Top card from a sequence of three or more cards headed by the ten or higher (e.g., from K-Q-J-5, lead the king; from J-10-9-8, lead the jack). The top five cards in each suit (A, K, Q, J, 10) are called the 'honour cards'. Lead top of a sequence only when the sequence has one or more honours.

Lead fourth-highest (fourth from the top) if the long suit has no 3-card or longer sequence (e.g., from K-J-8-4-3, lead the 4).

PRE-BRIDGE GAME 2 — TRUMPS WHIST

Each player receives 13 cards. The top card of the other pack is turned up as the trump suit. This card is left face-up during the play to remind each of the players which suit is trumps. There is still no bidding and no dummy.

In trumps, a trick without a trump card is won by the highest card of the suit led, but a trick with a trump card is won by the highest trump.

You are still obliged to follow suit. If unable to follow suit at trumps, you are permitted to 'ruff' (i.e., play a trump card — to ruff simply means to trump). However, you are not obliged to do so and you may choose to discard a worthless card instead of ruffing. Since you are not forced to ruff when you are out of a suit, you will decide whether to ruff or whether to discard. It is sensible to ruff a winning card played by an opponent but it might be unwise to ruff if partner's card is going to win the trick anyway. Remember, you are partners.

Scoring: The trick score in trumps for each trick over six is:

30 points if spades or hearts are trumps.

20 points if diamonds or clubs are trumps.

If hearts are trumps, making 1♡ (7 tricks) is worth 30, 2♡ (8 tricks) is worth 60, 3♡ (9 tricks) is 90, 4♡ (10 tricks) is 120, and so on. If clubs are trumps, 7 tricks (1♣) would score 20, 8 tricks (2♣) scores 40, 9 tricks (3♣) is 60 and so on.

Strategy at trumps

Choose a short suit such as a singleton (one card in a suit) or a doubleton (two cards in a suit — lead top card from a doubleton) or a strong suit (headed by a sequence or by A-K). With none of these, a trump lead is reasonable with a lot of trumps (five or more) or start with the best of your other suits.

PRE-BRIDGE GAME 3 — TRUMPS AND NO-TRUMPS

Each player receives 13 cards. Opposite players are partners. The top card of the other pack is turned face up. If a 2, 3 or 4 is turned up, play no-trumps. If a higher card is turned up, the suit of the face-up card is trumps for that deal. This card is left face-up to remind the players of the trump suit or no-trumps.

The play and scoring is the same as Game 1 and 2. Game 3 is a combined version of Games 1 and 2.

Additional Strategy: Second player to a trick commonly plays low, giving partner a chance to win the trick. Playing low in second seat includes not ruffing when you have the chance to win by ruffing. If the earlier play has revealed that partner will be unable to win the trick, by all means play high or ruff in second seat to win the trick yourself.

Third player to a trick usually plays high, trying to win the trick if possible. If partner's card has already won the trick, you need not beat partner's card in third or fourth seat.

PRE-BRIDGE GAME 4 — DEALER'S WHIST

Each player receives 13 cards. The dealer, after examining the 13 cards held and without consulting partner, declares the trump suit or no-trumps. This gives the dealer some control over the selection of trumps, whereas in Games 2 and 3, the card turned up as trumps (or no-trumps) is purely a matter of luck. When you are dealer, it is best to choose only a suit with five or more cards as your trump suit. With no five-card or longer suit, usually prefer to choose no-trumps.

Play: Same as before. There is no dummy.

Scoring: Same as before.

PRE-BRIDGE GAME 5 — PARTNERSHIP WHIST

This is the same as Game 4 except that the dealer and dealer's partner discuss whether to play in trumps or no-trumps. This gives the dealer's side a much better chance of discovering a good trump suit than when the dealer alone makes the choice.

The dealer or dealer's partner each makes one suggestion ('bid') at a time, nominating a trump suit or no-trumps. The dealer makes the first bid. If partner agrees, that decides the trump suit or no-trumps. If partner disagrees, partner makes an alternative suggestion. If no trump suit is agreed after three turns each, the hand is to be played in no-trumps.

Play: Same as before. There is still no dummy.

Scoring: Same as before.

PRE-BRIDGE GAME 6 — DECLARER'S WHIST

Each player counts the high card points (HCP) for the top four cards in each suit, **A = 4, K = 3, Q = 2, J = 1**. Starting with the dealer, each player calls out the total number of points held. The player who has most points becomes the 'declarer'. If there is a tie for the most points held, the declarer will be the dealer (if involved in the tie) or the player nearest the dealer (if the dealer is not involved in the tie . . . nearest goes according to clockwise direction).

The rest of the game is the same as Game 4 except that the declarer (rather than the dealer) nominates what is to be trumps or whether play is to be at no-trumps.

Play: Same as before. There is still no dummy.

Scoring: Same as before.

GAME 7 — DUMMY WHIST WITHOUT POINTS

Each player receives 13 cards. *The partner of the dealer puts all 13 cards face up in suits on the table as the dummy hand.* The dealer studies the dummy cards, declares the trump suit or no-trumps and so becomes the declarer for that deal.

Choose as trumps a suit with eight or more cards in the combined hands. If more than one trump suit is available, choose a major suit (spades or hearts) rather than a minor suit (diamonds or clubs), as the majors score more, 30 per trick rather than just 20 per trick.

If the suits are both majors or both minors, choose the longer, or if both have the same length, go with the stronger, the one with more high cards. With no suit which has eight or more trumps together, usually choose no-trumps. Being able to see partner's hand gives the dealer's side an even better chance of finding no-trumps or the best suit for trumps.

After the trump suit or no-trumps has been declared, the player on the left of the declarer makes the first lead. The play proceeds as before but **the declarer must play both hands.** The dummy player takes no part in the play. If dummy wins a trick, the next lead comes from dummy, while if declarer wins a trick, declarer must lead to the next trick.

Scoring

Same as usual as long as declarer wins at least seven tricks. If declarer fails to win seven tricks or more, the other side (the 'defenders') score bonus points at the rate of 50 for each trick by which declarer failed. For example, if declarer made only four tricks, the other side would score 150 bonus points, since declarer failed ('went down') by three tricks.

Bonus points are scored above the line and do not count towards scoring a game. Only the declarer side can score points towards game. Bonus points are still valuable since they count as part of your total points at the end of the rubber.

PRE-BRIDGE GAME 8 — DUMMY WHIST

The players count their high card points, using **A = 4, K = 3, Q = 2, J = 1.** Starting with the dealer, each player calls out the total number of points held. The side which has more points becomes the declarer side and the partner that has more points becomes the declarer. Dummy is revealed and declarer nominates the trump suit or no-trumps. (The pack has 40 HCP. If each side has 20, the dealer's side becomes the declarer side. For a tie in the declarer side, the player nearer the dealer will be the declarer.)

The play proceeds as before: the player on the left of declarer makes the opening lead and declarer plays both the dummy cards and his own hand.

Scoring

If declarer scores seven tricks or more, scoring is as usual. If declarer fails to win seven tricks, the opponents score bonus points. Only *the declarer side can score points for game* (below the line). Where the declarer side has not won a game ('not vulnerable'), the opponents score 50 bonus points for each trick by which they defeated declarer, regardless of the trump suit or whether no-trumps is played. Where the declarer side has won a game ('vulnerable'), the opponents will score 100 points for each trick by which they have defeated declarer.

The existence of the dummy distinguishes Bridge from other trick-taking games. From the first lead, each player sees half the pack (13 cards in hand plus the 13 in dummy). This makes Bridge essentially a game of skill, in contrast to the large luck factor in other games. Since the declarer side here will have more points than the defenders, the declarer side is likely to succeed in taking seven or more tricks.

PRE-BRIDGE GAME 9 — BIDDING WHIST

Starting with the dealer, each player states the number of points held. The side with more points is the declarer side and the two partners discuss which suit shall be trumps or whether to play no-trumps. Each partner in turn suggests a trump suit or no-trumps until agreement is reached. This is the 'bidding' or the 'auction'. A bid is simply a suggestion to partner which suit you prefer as trumps or whether you prefer no-trumps.

A bid suit should have at least four cards. With no long suit and no void (no cards in a suit) and no singleton (one card in a suit), it is usually best to suggest no-trumps at once. If there is no early agreement and neither partner insists on a suit, one partner should suggest no-trumps. After agreement, the first player to suggest the trump suit (or no-trumps) is the declarer.

In the play, the player on the left of the declarer makes the opening lead *before seeing dummy*. After the lead, dummy's 13 cards are placed face up (in suits), facing declarer. Trumps go on dummy's right.

Scoring: Same as for Game 8.

GAME 10 — CONTRACT WHIST + BIDDING

The early play proceeds exactly as Game 9. However, instead of needing to win just seven or more tricks, the declarer is required to win a specific number of tricks depending on the total points held by declarer and dummy:

20-22 points: 7 or more tricks in no-trumps
8 or more tricks with a trump suit

23-25 points: 8 or more tricks in no-trumps
9 or more tricks with a trump suit

26-32 points: 9 or more tricks in no-trumps
10 or more tricks with ♠ or ♡ as trumps
11 or more tricks with ◊ or ♣ as trumps

33-36 points: 12 or more tricks

37-40 points: All 13 tricks

Play: The opening lead is made before dummy appears.

[22]

Scoring
The same as for Game 9, but to score points declarer must win the number of tricks stipulated or more. If not, the defenders score bonus points of 50 (declarer not vulnerable) or 100 (declarer vulnerable) for each trick by which declarer fails.

If declarer is required to win 12 tricks ('small slam') and does so, the declarer side scores an extra bonus of 500 when not vulnerable or 750 vulnerable. If declarer is required to win all 13 tricks ('grand slam') and does so, the declarer side scores an extra 1000 not vulnerable or 1500 vulnerable.

Chapter 2

OPENING THE BIDDING

How does the bidding operate?
The play is preceded by the bidding, also called 'the auction'. Just as in an auction an item goes to the highest bidder, so in the bridge auction each side tries to outbid the other for the right to play the hand. As only the declarer side can score points towards a game, each side endeavours to win the bidding in order to become the declarer side.

The dealer makes the first bid, then the player on dealer's left and so on in clockwise rotation. Each player may pass (say 'No Bid') or make a bid. A player who has passed previously may bid later. A bid consists of a number (1, 2, 3, 4, 5, 6 or 7) followed by a suit or by no-trumps, for example, 3 Diamonds, 2 Spades, 4 Hearts, 7 No-trumps, and so on. 'No-trumps' means that there is to be no trump suit on the deal. Whenever a bid is made, the bidder is stating the number of tricks *above six* intended to be won in the play. The minimum number of tricks that you may bid for is seven. A bid of 1 Club contracts to make seven tricks with clubs as trumps. The number in the bid is the number of tricks to be won *over and above six*. (Six tricks is not even halfway and you must bid for more than half the tricks.) The final bid is called the 'contract'.

How many tricks must declarer win to succeed in each of the following contracts? Which suit is to be trumps?

(a) 3 Clubs (b) 4 Spades (c) 6 No-Trumps (d) 2 Diamonds

(*Answers:* (a) 9, clubs (b) 10, spades (c) 12, none (d) 8, diamonds)

If all pass without a bid on the first round, there is no play, the cards are thrown in and the next dealer deals a new hand. After a bid on the first round, the auction has started and will be won by the side that bids higher. The auction ends when a bid is followed by three passes. If you make a bid and the other three players pass, you are not allowed to bid again. Your last bid is the contract. The final bid (the contract) sets the trump suit (or no-trumps) and the number of tricks to be won by declarer in the play. The member of the declarer side who first bid the trump suit (or no-trumps) is the declarer.

After a bid, any player in turn may make a *higher* bid. A bid is higher than a previous bid if it is a higher number than the previous bid (three-anything is higher than two-anything) or if it is the same number but in a higher ranking denomination.

The order of ranking is:

NT	No-trumps
♠	Spades
♡	Hearts
◇	Diamonds
♣	Clubs

A bid of 1 Heart is higher than a bid of 1 Club. Likewise, a bid of 1 Spade is higher than a bid of 1 Heart. To bid spades after a bid of 2 No-trumps, you need to bid at least 3 Spades. A bid of 2 Spades, lower than 2 No-trumps, is insufficient.

(a) What is the highest bid possible?
(b) How many tricks does it undertake to make?
(c) What is the lowest bid possible?
(d) If the previous bid was 1 Spade, and you want to bid diamonds, what is the lowest bid in diamonds you can make?
(e) The previous bid was 1 Spade. Would a bid of 1 Heart be legal? What about a bid of 1 No-trump?

(*Answers:* (a) 7 No-trumps (b) 13 (c) 1 Club (d) 2 Diamonds (e) No; Yes)

[25]

Counting points

To succeed as the declarer side, you must win the number of tricks for which you have bid, or more. The more tricks in your contract, the harder your task. The strength of your hand is measured by the Point Count Method and whenever you make a bid, part of the message to your partner is the number of points you hold. The higher the contract, the more points you and partner need for success. The challenge in bidding is to assess your own points accurately and to gauge partner's points from the bids partner makes so that you can judge how high to bid. The basic count is high card points (HCP):

$$A = 4, \quad K = 3, \quad Q = 2, \quad J = 1$$

Each suit contains A-K-Q-J, 10 HCP. Thus, there are 40 HCP in the pack. As these 40 HCP are shared among the four players, an average hand has 10 HCP.

Bidding for game

When holding 26 points or more between you and partner, the partnership should bid a game. (A game bid is one which scores 100 points or more: 3NT, 4♠, 4♡, 5◊ and 5♣.) It is sound strategy not to pass in the bidding until some game is reached if the partnership *could* have 26 points or more.

With 26 points together, game is a good chance.
With 25 points together, game is a reasonable chance.
With 24 points or less, game prospects are poor.

Opening the bidding

An opening bid is the first bid in the auction. Pass is not a bid.
The standard approach for opening is:

0-11 points: Do not open the bidding. Pass initially.
12-19 points: Bid 1-of-a-suit, unless the hand fits 1NT.
20-up: Bid 2-of-a-suit, unless suitable for 2NT or 3NT.

Opening 2-of-a-suit, 2NT and 3NT are covered in Chapter 5.

PRE-BRIDGE GAME 11 — BIDDING MADE EASY

Each player receives 13 cards. Starting with the dealer, each player will either pass (say 'No Bid') or make a bid.

These are the rules for opening the bidding in this game:

1. With 0-11 points, pass initially. You may bid later.

2. With 12-19 points, bid a suit at the 1-level. If an opponent has already opened, a bid by you is an overcall (Chapter 6). You may overcall in a strong suit at the cheapest level.

3. With 20 points or more, open with a suit bid at the 2-level.

4. In this game only, you are not permitted to bid no-trumps at your first turn, but may bid no-trumps at your second or later turn. Any suit that you bid must contain at least four cards.

If your partner has already opened the bidding, you are the responder and the guide for responding is:

1. With 0-5 points, pass an opening bid at the 1-level, but answer an opening bid of two, even with a worthless hand.

2. With 6 or more points, answer partner's opening bid either by supporting partner's suit or by bidding your own suit. Any suit you bid must contain at least four cards and support for partner's suit also requires four cards. In this game only, you are not permitted to bid no-trumps at your first turn, but you may bid no-trumps at your second or later turn.

3. With 16 or more points, reply with a jump in a new suit.

When you have more than one suit to bid, choose your first bid as follows, whether you are opener or responder:

1. Bid your longest suit first (not necessarily the strongest).

2. With two five-card suits, bid the higher-ranking suit first (spades is highest, then hearts, diamonds, clubs).

3. If you have only one four-card suit, bid that suit. With two or three four-card suits, bid the cheapest possible suit.

The bidding ends when a bid is followed by three passes. If you can work out that your side has at least 26 points, bid to 3NT, 4♠, 4♡, 5♦ and 5♣ (game). Choose a trump contract with eight or more trumps together. The declarer side is the one which makes the final bid (the contract) and the declarer is the member of that partnership who bid the trump suit or no-trumps first. The play proceeds as usual: left of declarer makes the opening lead, declarer plays own hand plus dummy.

Scoring

As normal if declarer makes the number of tricks required in the contract. If declarer fails to win the number of tricks required, the opponents score bonus points (50 per trick by which declarer fell short if declarer is not vulnerable, 100 per trick short if declarer is vulnerable).

PRE-BRIDGE GAME 12 - BIDDING WITH NO-TRUMPS

This game is identical to the previous except that you may open with a bid of 1NT with 12-14 points and no short suit and you may answer 1NT to partner's opening bid with 6-9 points and no good suit to bid.

Hand patterns and hand shapes

The 'pattern' of your 13 cards is described by the number of cards from the longest suit to the shortest suit. For example, a 6-4-2-1 pattern means the hand contains a six-card suit, a four-card suit, a doubleton and a singleton.

Give the patterns of these hands:

1.	♠ A 8 5 3	2.	♠ J 2	3.	♠ K 6 4
	♡ - - -		♡ A J 8 7 4 3		♡ 9 5 2
	♦ K Q 7 6 3		♦ 8 5 4		♦ A J 9
	♣ A K 9 8		♣ 3 2		♣ J 6 5 4

(*Answers:* 1: 5-4-4-0; 2: 6-3-2-2; 3: 4-3-3-3)

There are three hand shapes, balanced, semi-balanced and unbalanced.

Balanced shape: The three balanced patterns are, in order of frequency, 4-4-3-2, 5-3-3-2 or 4-3-3-3. These are hands with no void, no singleton and at most one doubleton.

Semi-balanced shape: The three semi-balanced patterns, in order of frequency, are 5-4-2-2, 6-3-2-2 or 7-2-2-2. These hands have no void, no singleton and two or three doubletons.

Unbalanced shape: These include all patterns other than those listed above. Every unbalanced hand has at least one singleton or one void.

Balanced hands are usually best for no-trumps, while unbalanced hands are usually best for a trump contract, provided that a good trump suit is available. Semi-balanced hands are reasonable for no-trumps but may also end up in a trump contract if a good trump suit is available.

How many suits do I have for bidding?

A one-suiter contains only one suit of four or more cards (e.g., 4-3-3-3, 5-3-3-2, 6-3-3-1, 7-3-2-1 patterns). A two-suiter contains two suits to bid, each of which has four or more cards (e.g., 5-4-2-2, 5-5-2-1, 6-4-3-0 patterns). A three-suiter has three suits with at least four cards (the 4-4-4-1 and 5-4-4-0 patterns). A suit to bid should contain at least four cards.

For the hands at the bottom of page 28, what is the shape of each hand and how many suits are available for bidding?

(*Answers:* 1: Unbalanced 3-suiter;   2: Semi-balanced 1-suiter;
3: Balanced 1-suiter)

Which opening bid should I choose?

With fewer than 12 points, pass. With 20 points or more, see Chapter 5 for your opening bid. With 12 to 19 points, the following rules will guide you to the correct opening bid:

The 1NT opening shows 12-14 points and balanced shape.
If the hand fits, prefer 1NT to any other opening bid.
If the hand does not fit a 1NT opening:

Bid your longest suit first.
If you have two or three suits of equal length:

With two five-card suits or two six-card suits (5-5 or 6-6 patterns), bid the higher-ranking suit first.

With four-card suits only and too strong for 1NT:

With a 4-3-3-3 pattern, bid your 4-card suit.

With a 4-4-3-2 pattern, bid your cheaper 4-card suit.

With a 4-4-4-1 and a red singleton, open with the suit ranking below the singleton, but with a black singleton, open the middle 4-card suit.

Examples of opening bids

♠ 7 6 2
♡ A K 8 3 2
♢ K Q 9
♣ K 8

You hold 15 HCP and a 5-3-3-2 pattern. The hand is a balanced one-suiter. You have more than enough to open the bidding. Open 1 Heart.

♠ A Q 8 3 2
♡ K 9 8 2
♢ 8
♣ K 8 4

You hold 12 HCP and a 5-4-3-1 pattern, an unbalanced two-suiter. Open 1 Spade, the longer suit first. If spades are not supported, bid the hearts next.

♠ A J 7 5
♡ K Q 9 2
♢ 8
♣ A K Q 5

You hold 19 HCP and a 4-4-4-1 pattern, an unbalanced three-suiter. Open 1 Club, the suit below your singleton when you hold a 4-4-4-1 with a red singleton.

♠ A 9 8 4
♡ K 7
♢ A J 7 6
♣ 8 3 2

You hold 12 HCP and a 4-4-3-2 pattern. The hand is a balanced two-suiter. Open 1 No-trump. When the hand fits, prefer 1 No-trump to any other opening.

♠ A 9 8 4   You hold 16 HCP and a 4-4-3-2 pattern, a
♡ K 7   balanced two-suiter too strong for 1NT. Start
◇ A J 7 6   with 1 Diamond, the cheaper four-card suit.
♣ A 3 2   This is known as bidding 'up the line'.

♠ J 8 6 3 2   You hold 18 HCP and a 5-4-3-1 pattern,
♡ 7   an unbalanced two-suiter. Open 1 Spade,
◇ A K Q J   the longer suit first. The diamonds will be
♣ A K 2   winners even if spades become trumps.

♠ A K 8   You hold 17 HCP and a 4-3-3-3 pattern, a
♡ K Q 10   balanced one-suiter. The 4-3-3-3 pattern is
◇ A J 10   called a 'flat' hand. Open 1 Club. The poor
♣ 5 4 3 2   quality of the suit is not important.

♠ Q 9 7 6 2   You hold 13 HCP and a 5-5-2-1 pattern,
♡ A K Q 5 4 an unbalanced two-suiter. Open 1 Spade,
◇ Q 3   the higher suit with a 5-5 pattern. The
♣ 10   better quality of the hearts changes nothing.

♠ K Q 8 6 3   You hold 14 HCP and a 6-5-2-0 pattern, a
♡ - - -   freak two-suiter. Open 1 Club, your longer
◇ A 9   suit first. You can show the spades on the
♣ K Q 7 4 3 2 next round of bidding.

A little about bridge notation

Bridge bids are written number first, suit next, so that 1♠
stands for 1 Spade, 1NT means 1 No-Trump, 4♡ is 4 Hearts,
2◇ is 2 Diamonds, 6♣ is 6 Clubs, and so on. Cards are written
with the suit symbol first, card next. The ♠J represents the
jack of spades, ♡4 stands for the 4 of hearts, ◇9 is the 9 of
diamonds, ♣2 is the 2 of clubs, and so on.

[31]

Example hands

(Play hands can be made up by using pages 92-95.)

Hand 1: Dealer North : Nil vulnerable

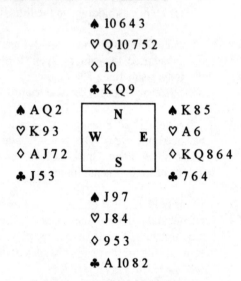

```
                    ♠ 10 6 4 3
                    ♡ Q 10 7 5 2
                    ◇ 10
                    ♣ K Q 9
  ♠ A Q 2          ┌─────────┐        ♠ K 8 5
  ♡ K 9 3          │    N    │        ♡ A 6
  ◇ A J 7 2        │ W     E │        ◇ K Q 8 6 4
  ♣ J 5 3          │    S    │        ♣ 7 6 4
                   └─────────┘
                    ♠ J 9 7
                    ♡ J 8 4
                    ◇ 9 5 3
                    ♣ A 10 8 2
```

RECOMMENDED BIDDING

West	North	East	South
	No	1NT	No
3NT	No	No	No

Bidding: West can judge East-West have at least 27 points.

Lead: 2 of clubs, fourth-highest from the long suit.

Play: North-South should win the first four tricks in clubs
(♣Q; ♣K; ♣A; ♣10). Declarer should win the rest with plenty
of winners available in spades, hearts and diamonds. It is
worth noting that 5◇ would fail despite the nine-card trump
fit. Balanced hands are usually best played in no-trumps.

Hand 2: Dealer East : North-South vulnerable

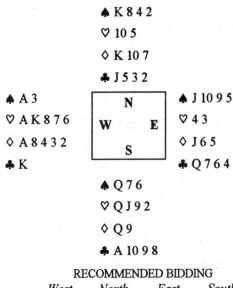

```
                    ♠ K 8 4 2
                    ♡ 10 5
                    ♦ K 10 7
                    ♣ J 5 3 2
  ♠ A 3              ┌─────────┐        ♠ J 10 9 5
  ♡ A K 8 7 6       │    N    │        ♡ 4 3
  ♦ A 8 4 3 2       │ W     E │        ♦ J 6 5
  ♣ K               │    S    │        ♣ Q 7 6 4
                    └─────────┘
                    ♠ Q 7 6
                    ♡ Q J 9 2
                    ♦ Q 9
                    ♣ A 10 9 8
```

RECOMMENDED BIDDING

West	North	East	South
		No	No
1♡	No	No	No

Bidding: West opens the higher of two five-card suits. East is too weak to respond — East-West cannot have 26 points. As neither North nor South is worth a bid, West is left in 1♡.

Lead: North has no attractive lead. The 2 of spades, fourth-highest, is as good as anything.

Play: South plays the queen of spades (third-hand-high) and West wins with the ace. The ace and king of hearts should be cashed followed by the ace of diamonds and another diamond. West continues with diamonds at every opportunity and should make seven tricks.

[33]

Hand 3: Dealer South : East-West vulnerable

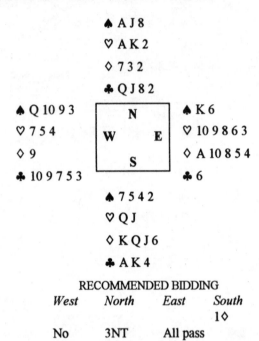

♠ A J 8
♡ A K 2
◇ 7 3 2
♣ Q J 8 2

♠ Q 10 9 3
♡ 7 5 4
◇ 9
♣ 10 9 7 5 3

♠ K 6
♡ 10 9 8 6 3
◇ A 10 8 5 4
♣ 6

♠ 7 5 4 2
♡ Q J
◇ K Q J 6
♣ A K 4

RECOMMENDED BIDDING

West	North	East	South
			1◇
No	3NT	All pass	

Bidding: South bids the cheaper four-card suit. North has more than enough for game, a flat hand and every suit outside diamonds well covered, making 3NT a logical choice.

Lead: 10 of hearts, top of sequence. Do not lead a diamond. One usually avoids leading a suit bid by the opponents.

Play: North can count eight instant winners (one spade trick, three hearts, four clubs). The diamonds can provide at least two more tricks, but first the ◇A must be dislodged. Win the ♡Q and lead the ◇K. Set up your extra tricks *before* cashing your sure winners

[34]

Hand 4: Dealer West : Both vulnerable

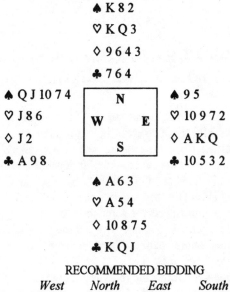

```
                    ♠ K 8 2
                    ♡ K Q 3
                    ◊ 9 6 4 3
                    ♣ 7 6 4
  ♠ Q J 10 7 4        N          ♠ 9 5
  ♡ J 8 6        W         E     ♡ 10 9 7 2
  ◊ J 2                           ◊ A K Q
  ♣ A 9 8              S          ♣ 10 5 3 2
                    ♠ A 6 3
                    ♡ A 5 4
                    ◊ 10 8 7 5
                    ♣ K Q J
```

RECOMMENDED BIDDING

West	North	East	South
No	No	No	1NT
No	No	No	

Bidding: South has a sound 1NT opening with 14 points and a flat hand. North knows North-South cannot have 26 points.

Lead: Queen of spades, top of sequence from your long suit.

Play: South can count five sure tricks (two spades and three hearts). Two extra tricks can be set up in clubs but to do so the ace of clubs must be knocked out. Declarer should win the spade lead and immediately lead clubs. Set up your extra tricks before cashing your sure winners. If South played the top spades and hearts before starting on the clubs, the defenders would be able to defeat 1NT.

[35]

Chapter 3

WEAK HAND RESPONSES
TO A ONE-OPENING

As 10 points is an average hand, below 10 is considered weak. You do not usually bid if so weak unless partner has already bid. When partner opens the bidding, you might make a game with fewer than 10 points as responder. It depends on opener's strength and the number of points held by responder. Weak responding hands are divided into two ranges, 0-5 and 6-9.

With 0-5 points, prospects for game are too slim, but with 6 points or better, game is possible with a strong trump fit or if opener has a maximum opening. The principles therefore are:

Responder has 0-5 points: pass.

Responder has 6-9 points: bid (but keep it low!).

The response chosen will depend on the opening bid. Responding to 1NT is not the same as responding to a suit opening since opener's point count is different, with the 1NT opening being 12-14 and suit openings being 12-19.

After a 1NT opening, game is unlikely if responder has 6-10 points. With a balanced hand up to 10 points, pass the 1NT opening. With an unbalanced hand or a long suit, responder should choose a trump part-score rather than 1NT. Even though game has little chance, it is worth responding when you have a long suit. It makes sense to play the part-score that has the best chance of success. With such a hand, respond to 1NT with a suit at the two-level, promising at least five cards in the suit bid and a weak responding hand.

After a 1♣, 1♦, 1♥ or 1♠ opening, a responding hand of 6-9 points is no cause for celebration. Opener may have just 12 points, giving the partnership barely half the points in the pack. If weak, keep the bidding at a low level. You may support opener's suit by raising it to the two-level (e.g., 1♥ : 2♥), but otherwise make a bid only at the one-level (e.g., 1♥ : 1♠). With 6-9 points responder should certainly bid, since opener might have 20 points. Then a game contract may be a decent chance. However, if opener has only 12 points or so, it will be tough to make more than seven or eight tricks, and so it pays to be conservative with just 6-9 points. The guideline is:

With 6-9 points, raise opener's suit to the two-level or respond at the one-level in a suit or 1NT. Do not bid a new suit at the two-level with less than 10 points.

With a choice of actions, the guidelines for responder are:

Raise opener's major suit.
Raise opener's minor suit if you have no major suit to bid.
Bid one in your own suit (longest first; with 5-5 or 6-6 shape, bid the higher suit; bid the cheapest with only 4-card suits).
Bid 1NT if none of the above is available.

A bid suit need not be strong but it must contain at least four cards. This enables partner to see whether a decent trump fit exists (at least eight trumps together). A suit bid once promises at least a four-card suit. To support this suit, you need four trumps to ensure an eight-card fit. This applies both to responder supporting opener and to opener supporting responder.

When you are supporting partner's suit, voids, singletons and doubletons become valuable because you are able to trump once you run out of a suit. The shorter your holding in a suit outside trumps, the more valuable your support and you should count extra points for shortages when supporting partner or when partner has supported you. The Short Suit Count is:

$$\text{Void} \quad = \quad \text{5 points}$$
$$\text{Singleton} \quad = \quad \text{3 points}$$
$$\text{Doubleton} \quad = \quad \text{1 point}$$

The 5-3-1 count is added only after a trump fit is known. Add these ruffing points for each shortage held, for example, add 6 points for two singletons or 2 points for two doubletons.

Examples of weak hand responses

♠ K 6 4 2
♡ 8 7
◊ 6 5 3
♣ 7 6 4 2

You hold only 3 points and should pass any opening bid from 1♣ to 1NT. Even if partner opened 1♠, your hand is worth only 4 points (one for the doubleton).

♠ A 7 2
♡ 6 5 4
◊ Q 9 5 3
♣ 7 4 3

You should pass 1NT (no chance for game), but respond to any other 1-opening. Over 1♣, bid 1◊. Over 1◊, raise to 2◊. Over 1♡ or 1♠, bid 1NT.

♠ Q 10 8 4 2
♡ K 2
◊ 7 5
♣ J 5 3 2

Over 1NT, bid 2♠, promising at least five spades. Over 1♣, 1◊ or 1♡, bid 1♠ (show the spades rather than raise the clubs). Over 1♠, raise to 2♠.

♠ A 9 8 2
♡ K J 6 5
◊ 8 7
♣ 7 6 2

Over 1NT, you should pass (game is highly unlikely). Over 1♣ or 1◊, bid 1♡ (bid four-card suits 'up-the-line'). Raise 1♡ to 2♡ and raise 1♠ to 2♠.

Rebids by the opener

Opener judges whether the partnership has enough for game. Your requirements are :

For 3NT, about 26 points between you.

For 4♠ or 4♡, at least 8 trumps and 26 points between you.

For 5◊ or 5♣, at least 8 trumps and 29 points between you.

If the partnership might have 26 points, opener keeps on bidding. If opener can tell that 26 points together is impossible opener may pass if satisfied with responder's last bid. If opener dislikes responder's last suggestion, opener may make some other bid even though the partnership cannot have 26 points.

♠ A J 8 4 3   You opened 1♠, partner responded 1NT
♡ K 9 7 5 4   (6-9 points). The partnership does not
♦ A 6   hold 26 points, but you dislike no-trumps
♣ J   because of your unbalanced hand.

Do not pass 1NT. Bid 2♡, telling partner you would rather play in spades or in hearts. Responder passes 2♡ if hearts are preferred, but rebids 2♠ if he likes spades better.

If opener can tell that the partnership has 26 points, the opener can bid game if certain of the correct game contract (remembering that a good trump suit requires at least eight trumps together) or can make a jump rebid (a jump is a bid of one more than necessary) to indicate a strong hand.

♠ A Q 6   You opened 1♦, partner responded 1NT
♡ A J 8   (6-9 points). A quick calculation tells you
♦ K J 10 3   the partnership has 25 points, perhaps
♣ K J 8   more. Take a shot at 3NT.

♠ A Q 7 3   You opened 1♡. What is your rebid if
♡ A K 9 7 2   partner responds (a) 2♡? (b) 1♠?
♦ A Q   You know partner has at least 6 points.
♣ 5 2   You are worth 21 points, counting one
               for each doubleton.

You can also tell in each case that the partnership has a good trump fit, so rebid 4 Hearts in (a) and 4 Spades in (b).

There are two important principles for opener's rebid:

(1) If responder bids a new suit, opener must bid again. Responder's change of suit is said to be a 'forcing bid'.

(2) With a minimum opening (less than 16 points), opener should rebid at the cheapest level if unable or unwilling to pass responder's bid. Minimum bids show minimum hands, jump bids show strong hands.

For opener's rebid, opener may choose any of these actions:

Raise responder's suit with four trumps in support.

Bid no-trumps with a balanced hand.

Bid a new suit with at least four cards in that suit.

Bid the first suit again if it is at least five cards long.

When bid initially, a suit may have only four cards. If bid again, it must contain at least five cards. If bid for a third time, it would be at least six cards long. This helps partner decide whether the partnership has eight or more trumps.

There are two ways responder can deduce that opener holds at least a five card suit. One is where opener bids the same suit again. Rebidding a suit promises at least five cards in the suit. Another is when opener's *second* bid is in a new suit lower-ranking than opener's first suit. Opener then figures to have at least five cards in the first suit. This follows from the rule that four-card suits are normally bid up-the-line, cheaper suit first.

Suppose opener has bid 1♠ and after your reply of 1NT, opener rebids 2♣. (Incidentally, in bridge notation, this would be written as 1♠ : 1NT, 2♣.) You can tell that if opener is bidding correctly, opener will have at least five spades and at least four clubs, because if opener had only *four* spades and four clubs, the correct opening would be 1♣ and not 1♠.

If opener has bid suits 'up-the-line' at the one-level, such as
1◊ : 1♡, 1♠, opener may have just four-card suits but if
opener bids suits 'down-the-line' (e.g., 1♡ : 1♠, 2◊), opener
will have at least five cards in the first suit and four or more
cards in the second bid suit.

Examples of opener's rebids

♠ A J 7 2	You opened 1◊ and have a minimum
♡ 9 3	opening. If partner responds 1♡, rebid
◊ A Q J 4 3	1♠. Raise a 1♠ response to 2♠. If partner
♣ J 9	raises 1◊ to 2◊, opener should pass.

Over a 1NT response, rebid 2◊. There is little point in
bidding 2♠ since there are no reasonable prospects for game
and partner does not have a spade suit. Partner would have bid
1♠ to show the major suit rather than respond 1NT.

♠ A K 8 6	You opened 1◊ and have a good hand.
♡ 7	Over a 1♡ response, rebid 1♠. You are
◊ A Q J 6 2	not certain of the best spot yet.
♣ K 4 3	

Over 1♠, raise to 4♠. You are sure spades is the best suit and
you are worth 20 points with spades as trumps because of your
singleton. Over a response of 1NT or 2◊, rebid 2♠. There are
chances for game and while partner does not have length in
spades, your best move is to describe your hand and indicate
better than a minimum opening. Partner should realise you are
strong. With a minimum, you would not bid beyond 2◊.

♠ A 9 4 3	You opened 1♣ on your three-suiter.
♡ A J 8 6	Over a reply of 1◊, rebid 1♡ ('up-the-
◊ - - -	line'). Over 1♡ or 1♠, jump to 4♡/4♠
♣ A Q 6 3 2	(the void makes your hand worth 20).

[41]

♠ A Q 7
♡ K Q 2
◇ 8 7 3
♣ K J 7 2

You opened 1♣ with 15 HCP, a modest balanced hand. If partner replies 1◇ or 1♡ or 1♠, you should rebid 1NT. If partner replies 1NT or 2♣, pass.

♠ A Q 7
♡ A J 8
◇ A J 4
♣ Q 9 6 3

You opened 1♣ with 18 HCP, a strong balanced hand. If partner replies 1◇ or 1♡ or 1♠, jump rebid to 2NT. If partner responds 1NT or 2♣, rebid 2NT.

♠ A
♡ 8 7 2
◇ Q J 3
♣ A Q 9 7 4 2

You opened 1♣ and have a minimum, unbalanced one-suiter. Over 1◇ or 1♡ or 1♠ or 1NT, rebid 2♣. Over a raise to 2♣, pass. Prospects for game are too remote.

♠ A
♡ 8 7 2
◇ A Q 3
♣ A Q J 7 4 2

You opened 1♣ and have a strong, unbalanced one-suiter. Over 1◇ or 1♡ or 1♠ or 1NT, make a jump rebid to 3♣. Over a raise to 2♣, raise again to 3♣.

Examples of responder's rebids

♠ A 7
♡ Q 7 3
◇ Q 9 6 5 2
♣ 8 7 6

Imagine partner opened 1♣ to which you responded 1◇. If opener rebids 1♡ or 1♠, you should rebid 1NT. If opener rebids 1NT or 2♣, you should pass.

♠ J 3
♡ K 8 7 6 5 2
◇ J 6
♣ J 3 2

Partner opened 1♣ and you responded 1♡. Over a rebid of 1♠ or 1NT, you should rebid 2♡. Over opener's rebid of 2♣ or 2♡, you should pass.

♠ A 8 7
♡ K 8 4 3
◇ Q 9 7
♣ 6 5 2

Partner opened 1♣ and you responded 1♡. Over 1♠, bid 1NT. Over 1NT, 2♣ or 2♡, you should pass. Over any strong rebid by opener, you should bid to game.

[42]

Example hands

(Play hands can be made up by using pages 92-95.)

Hand 5: Dealer North : North-South vulnerable

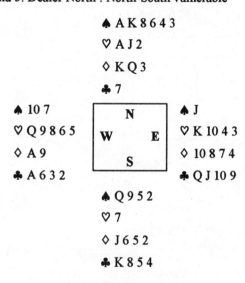

```
                    ♠ A K 8 6 4 3
                    ♡ A J 2
                    ◊ K Q 3
                    ♣ 7
    ♠ 10 7                          ♠ J
    ♡ Q 9 8 6 5      N              ♡ K 10 4 3
    ◊ A 9         W     E           ◊ 10 8 7 4
    ♣ A 6 3 2       S              ♣ Q J 10 9
                    ♠ Q 9 5 2
                    ♡ 7
                    ◊ J 6 5 2
                    ♣ K 8 5 4
```

RECOMMENDED BIDDING

West	North	East	South
	1♠	No	2♠
No	4♠	All pass	

Bidding: After receiving the raise, North revalues to 20 points (adding 3 for a singleton after trump support). With South's 6-9, North has enough for game and bids it at once.

Lead: ♣Q. Top of sequence is a very attractive start.

Play: North should ruff the second round of clubs and draw trumps in two rounds. Declarer then leads the ◊K to knock out the ace and set up extra winners there. Later cash the ♡A and ruff the two heart losers in dummy. Making eleven tricks.

[43]

Hand 6: Dealer East : East-West vulnerable

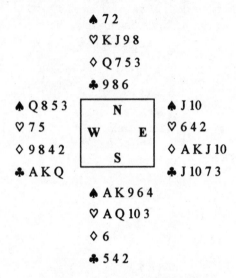

```
                    ♠ 7 2
                    ♡ K J 9 8
                    ◊ Q 7 5 3
                    ♣ 9 8 6
    ♠ Q 8 5 3      ┌─────────┐      ♠ J 10
    ♡ 7 5          │    N    │      ♡ 6 4 2
    ◊ 9 8 4 2      │ W     E │      ◊ A K J 10
    ♣ A K Q        │    S    │      ♣ J 10 7 3
                   └─────────┘
                    ♠ A K 9 6 4
                    ♡ A Q 10 3
                    ◊ 6
                    ♣ 5 4 2
```

RECOMMENDED BIDDING

West	North	East	South
		No	1♠
No	1NT	No	2♡
No	No	No	

Bidding: North dislikes spades and responds 1NT (6-9). South, not keen on no-trumps, shows the second suit with 2♡. North prefers hearts to spades and therefore passes 2♡.

Lead: West cashes the club winners.

Play: After three rounds of clubs, West should switch to a diamond, the unbid suit. When South gains the lead, South should cash the ♠A, ♠K and continue by ruffing spades in dummy and diamonds in hand, a cross-ruff to make nine tricks. A cross-ruff allows you to win your trumps separately.

[44]

Hand 7: Dealer South : Both vulnerable

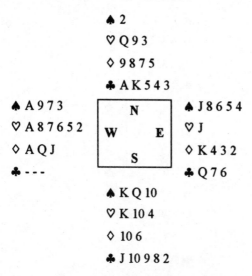

```
                    ♠ 2
                    ♡ Q 9 3
                    ◇ 9 8 7 5
                    ♣ A K 5 4 3
  ♠ A 9 7 3          N          ♠ J 8 6 5 4
  ♡ A 8 7 6 5 2   W     E       ♡ J
  ◇ A Q J            S          ◇ K 4 3 2
  ♣ - - -                       ♣ Q 7 6
                    ♠ K Q 10
                    ♡ K 10 4
                    ◇ 10 6
                    ♣ J 10 9 8 2
```

RECOMMENDED BIDDING

West	North	East	South
			No
1♡	No	1♠	No
4♠	No	No	No

Bidding: After East responds 1♠, West revalues. With five for the void, West is worth 20 points and as East has shown 6 points at least, West can count enough to bid game.

Lead: Jack of clubs, top of sequence.

Play: Ruff the club in dummy and play the ♠A. Leave the two top trumps out and cash ♡A, ruff a heart, ruff a club, ruff a heart and ruff a club. Play the diamond winners and make eleven tricks, losing only two trump tricks. If declarer leads a second trump at trick 3, the defenders can beat 4♠.

Hand 8: Dealer West : Nil vulnerable

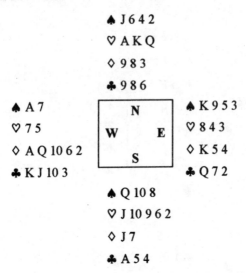

♠ J 6 4 2
♡ A K Q
♦ 9 8 3
♣ 9 8 6

♠ A 7
♡ 7 5
♦ A Q 10 6 2
♣ K J 10 3

♠ K 9 5 3
♡ 8 4 3
♦ K 5 4
♣ Q 7 2

♠ Q 10 8
♡ J 10 9 6 2
♦ J 7
♣ A 5 4

RECOMMENDED BIDDING

West	North	East	South
1♦	No	1♠	No
2♣	No	2♦	All pass

Bidding: East bids 1♠ showing four spades and 6 or more points. West does not like spades and rebids 2♣ to show the second suit. East bids 2♦ to show preference for diamonds and a weakish hand. With a strong hand, East would have bid 3♦.

Lead: North leads the heart winners.

Play: West ruffs the third heart and draws trumps in three rounds. Clubs are led to knock out the ♣A and declarer can make ten tricks. If East-West were to play no-trumps, the defence could take six tricks: three rounds of hearts and later the ♣A, followed by two more heart tricks from South.

[46]

Chapter 4

STRONG HAND RESPONSES TO A ONE-OPENING

Where responder has 10 or more points, prospects for game are good. If you know there are enough points for game and can tell the best contract, go ahead and bid it. For example:

♠ A J 7
♡ K 6 4
◇ 8 6 3 2
♣ A K 4

Partner opens 1NT and you hold this balanced hand. What is your response?

Adding your points to partner's, you have at least 27 points together. Bid 3NT.

Contrast this situation:

♠ A J 7 6 5 3
♡ 6
◇ A K J
♣ J 5 4

Partner opens 1NT and again you know the partnership has enough points for a game (your 14 + partner's 12 minimum). Your response?

This time your hand is not suitable for no-trumps because of the singleton. You can deduce that there must be at least eight spades in the partnership hands, as you have six and partner would not open 1NT with a singleton or a void. Therefore, you are in a position to bid to the correct contract of 4 Spades.

A lot of the time responder may not be certain that there are enough points for a game or may not be able to tell whether the partnership has eight of more trumps together. In such cases, responder will not be able to bid a game yet and will have to make some other bid to investigate the possibilities.

With a strong hand, 10 points or more, responder must avoid the weak response of 1NT or raising opener's suit to the two level. Bidding a new suit forces the opener to bid again and may be made with a powerful responding hand. A jump response in a new suit ('jump-shift') is a very strong action which insists on game being reached (a 'game-force' response).

Responding to 1NT

With 13 points or more, bid 3NT with a balanced hand or bid 4♡ or 4♠ with a six-card or longer suit. Add the 5-3-1 count when a known 8-card trump fit exists. A suit response at the three-level, e.g., 1NT : 3♣, shows 12 points or more (enough for game) and at least a five-card suit. Opener should support the suit with three trumps, else bid 3NT with a doubleton.

♠ A J 3	You have opened 1NT.
♡ K 2	What action do you take if partner
◊ 9 8 7 4	responds: (a) 3NT? (b) 4♠? (c) 4♡?
♣ A J 4 2	(d) 3♠? (e) 3♡?

As 3NT, 4♠ and 4♡ are games, you should pass in (a), (b) and (c). The 3♠ and 3♡ responses show five-card suits, so that opener should raise to 4♠ in (d) as there will be eight spades together, but rebid 3NT in (e) since you have only doubleton support for hearts.

Responding to 1-of-a-suit with 10 points or more:

The most common action is a change of suit initially. If you have a two-suiter or a three-suiter:

Bid your longest suit first.

With 5-5 or 6-6, bid the higher-ranking suit first.

With 4-card suits only, bid the cheapest ('up-the-line').

[48]

Specific responses

A response of 2NT to 1NT or to 1♣, 1◇, 1♡ or 1♠ shows a balanced hand of 11-12 points and also no four-card major. The response of 3NT to a suit opening shows 13-15 points and a 4-3-3-3 pattern with no major. Raising opener's suit from the 1-level to the 3-level (e.g., 1♣ : 3♣ or 1♡ : 3♡) shows 10-12 points and promises 4-card or better support for opener's suit.

If partner opened 1♣ or 1◇, prefer a major suit to a no-trump response or raising opener's minor. If partner opened 1♡ or 1♠, prefer to raise opener's major to any other response.

Rebids by opener

After a response in a new suit, opener must bid again. With support, opener should raise responder's major. If this is not possible, bid a new suit, or, if the hand is balanced, rebid in no-trumps. As a last resort, opener may rebid the first suit with five or more cards in that suit. A minimum rebid by opener shows a minimum opening, but a no-trump rebid will be 15-16 points and a jump-rebid in no-trumps shows 17 or more. Other jump-rebids by opener show a strong hand, better than a minimum 12-15 point opening.

Examples of strong responses

♠ A Q 7 3 2   Partner opens 1♣. You know you have
♡ A K 4 3   enough points for a game, but which
◇ 7 2   game? As you cannot tell yet, bid 1♠ for
♣ 8 6   the time being and await opener's rebid.

♠ A 7 6   Partner opens 1◇. With enough for a
♡ K 4 3   game and balanced shape, no-trumps is
◇ K 8 3   attractive. Respond 3NT showing 13-15
♣ K J 7 5   points and a 4-3-3-3 pattern.

♠ A K Q J 8 6
♡ A K 4
◇ 7 3
♣ Q 5

Whether partner opened 1♣, 1◇ or 1♡, you should respond 2♠, a jump in a new suit, called a 'jump-shift'. The jump-shift shows a strong suit and at least 16 HCP.

♠ 4 3
♡ 5
◇ A Q 8 5 2
♣ A K J 9 7

If partner opened 1♡ or 1♠, you should respond 2◇, the higher of two five-card suits. You have enough for a game, but which game is far from clear yet.

♠ A Q 9 2
♡ 7
◇ A J 10 3
♣ K J 7 4

If partner opened 1◇ or 1♡, respond 1♠, (up-the-line, the cheapest four-card suit). The points are there for a game but again you cannot tell which game is best.

Examples of opener's rebids

♠ A J 8 7 2
♡ K 9 4 3
◇ 7
♣ A Q 2

You opened 1♠ and partner responded 2NT (11-12 balanced). What is your rebid? Is the best game 4♠, 4♡ or 3NT? Bid 3♡ to say you prefer spades or hearts.

♠ 7
♡ K Q 8 7 6 2
◇ A J 10
♣ K J 3

You opened 1♡ and partner responded 2NT. Your best rebid is 4♡. You know you have enough for game and you know there are at least eight hearts together.

♠ K Q 9 8 3
♡ Q J 6 4 2
◇ 4
♣ A J

You opened 1♠, (five-card suits are bid 'down-the-line'), partner responded 2◇. You should rebid 2♡. Your destination is still not clear, so describe your hand.

♠ J 3
♡ A K 9 6
◇ Q J 3
♣ A J 7 5

You opened 1♣ (cheaper 4-card suit). If partner bids 2♠ (jump-shift), rebid 2NT. Had partner responded 1♠, you would have rebid 1NT.

♠ Q J 2
♡ K Q 9 8 6
◊ A J 4 3 2
♣ - - -

You opened 1♡ and partner responded 3♣ (jump-shift). You should rebid 3◊, just as you would rebid 2◊ if partner's response had been 2♣.

Examples of responder's rebids

♠ A Q 7 3 2
♡ A K 6 2
◊ 7 4
♣ 9 6

Partner opened 1♣, you responded 1♠. If partner rebids 2♣, you are still not sure of the best spot, so rebid 2♡. Had partner rebid 2♠, you would have bid 4♠.

♠ A J 5 3
♡ A J 8 7
◊ 4 3
♣ K J 3

Partner opened 1♣, you responded 1♡. If partner now rebids 1NT (15-16 points), bid 3NT, while if partner bids 2♡, bid 4♡ or if partner bids 1♠, raise to 4♠.

♠ 10
♡ 6 3 2
◊ A K 8 7 5
♣ A Q 9 4

Partner opened 1♠, you responded 2◊. If partner rebids 2♠, bid 3♣. If partner rebids 2♡, bid 3NT. Had partner opened 1♡ and rebid 2♡, you would now bid 4♡.

♠ A Q 8 7 4 2
♡ A 9 3
◊ 6
♣ 5 3 2

Partner opened 1◊, you responded 1♠. If partner rebids 1NT or raises to 2♠, bid 4♠, but if partner rebids 2♣ or 2◊, jump to 3♠, a strong invitation to game.

♠ A 10 9 7
♡ 7
◊ A J 7 5
♣ K Q 5 2

Partner opened 1♡, you responded 1♠. If partner now bids 1NT or 2♡, jump to 3NT, while over 2♣ or 2◊, you are worth a jump-raise to 4♣/4◊.

Example hands

(Play hands can be made up by using pages 92-95.)

Hand 9: Dealer North : E-W vulnerable

```
              ♠ K Q J 5 4 2
              ♡ A 8 3
              ◇ 7
              ♣ Q J 5
♠ 10 8 6          ┌─────────┐          ♠ 9
♡ K 9 4 2         │    N    │          ♡ Q J 10 7 5
◇ A J 10 6      W │         │ E        ◇ 9 3 2
♣ K 9            │    S    │          ♣ 10 8 7 3
                  └─────────┘
              ♠ A 7 3
              ♡ 6
              ◇ K Q 8 5 4
              ♣ A 6 4 2
```

RECOMMENDED BIDDING

West	North	East	South
	1♠	No	2◇
No	2♠	No	4♠
No	No	No	

Bidding: After 2♠, South knows there are enough spades as well as enough points to bid game in spades.

Lead: ♡Q. Top of sequence is easily the best here.

Play: Win ♡A and lead ◇7 to dummy's queen to set up a diamond trick. Later ruff the heart losers in dummy before drawing trumps. A club has to be lost but you make 11 tricks.

[52]

Hand 10: Dealer East : Both vulnerable

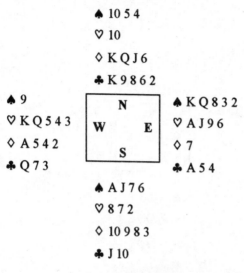

```
                    ♠ 10 5 4
                    ♡ 10
                    ◊ K Q J 6
                    ♣ K 9 8 6 2
♠ 9                                    ♠ K Q 8 3 2
♡ K Q 5 4 3         N                  ♡ A J 9 6
◊ A 5 4 2        W     E               ◊ 7
♣ Q 7 3             S                  ♣ A 5 4
                    ♠ A J 7 6
                    ♡ 8 7 2
                    ◊ 10 9 8 3
                    ♣ J 10
```

RECOMMENDED BIDDING

West	North	East	South
		1♠	No
2♡	No	4♡	All pass

Bidding: West's 2♡ showed at least 10 points (with only 6-9, raise partner or bid at the one-level). East is worth 17 points in hearts, counting 3 for the singleton, and so bids 4♡. With enough for game, do not dally — bid it.

Lead: ◊K, top of the strong sequence.

Play: Win ◊A and lead a spade to the king to set up the ♠Q as a winner. Before drawing trumps, ruff diamonds in dummy and discard a club loser on the ♠Q. Declarer can ruff diamonds in dummy and spades in hand. When you need to ruff several losers in dummy, do not draw trumps too early.

Hand 11: Dealer South : Nil vulnerable

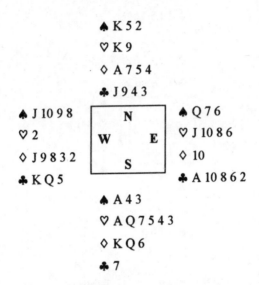

♠ K 5 2
♥ K 9
◇ A 7 5 4
♣ J 9 4 3

♠ J 10 9 8
♥ 2
◇ J 9 8 3 2
♣ K Q 5

♠ Q 7 6
♥ J 10 8 6
◇ 10
♣ A 10 8 6 2

♠ A 4 3
♥ A Q 7 5 4 3
◇ K Q 6
♣ 7

RECOMMENDED BIDDING

West	North	East	South
			1♥
No	2NT	No	4♥
No	No	No	

Bidding: North's 2NT shows 11-12 points, balanced shape. South knows there are enough points for game and at least eight hearts together. 3NT could be defeated on a club lead.

Lead: ♠J, top of sequence.

Play: Win the spade lead and draw trumps, starting with the ♥K. After three rounds of trumps, East has a trump winner. When there is one trump out, higher than yours, usually leave it out and play your other suits. Let them win their trump later.

[54]

Hand 12: Dealer West : North-South vulnerable

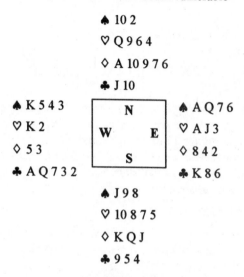

```
                        ♠ 10 2
                        ♡ Q 9 6 4
                        ◇ A 10 9 7 6
                        ♣ J 10
    ♠ K 5 4 3          ┌─────────┐          ♠ A Q 7 6
    ♡ K 2              │    N    │          ♡ A J 3
    ◇ 5 3              │ W     E │          ◇ 8 4 2
    ♣ A Q 7 3 2        │    S    │          ♣ K 8 6
                       └─────────┘
                        ♠ J 9 8
                        ♡ 10 8 7 5
                        ◇ K Q J
                        ♣ 9 5 4
```

RECOMMENDED BIDDING

West	North	East	South
1♣	No	1♠	No
2♠	No	4♠	All pass

Bidding: West opens 1♣, longest suit first, and East bids 1♠.
East intends to reach game but is not sure of the best spot.
3NT is a poor choice: the diamonds are so weak and East has
a major suit to show. Bid a major rather than respond in no-
trumps. Note that 3NT can be defeated on a diamond lead.

Lead: ◇K, top of sequence.

Play: Upon gaining the lead, East should draw trumps. You
can ruff a diamond loser in dummy or, preferably, discard
losers on the club winners by playing dummy's long suit *after*
drawing trumps. Making 11 tricks.

[55]

Chapter 5

SLAM BIDDING AND TWO-OPENINGS

The main aim of bidding is to reach a game if the partnership has enough points. The scoring also gives very substantial rewards for bidding for 12 or 13 tricks and then making your contract. A contract of six (12 tricks) is called a small slam and if you bid and make a small slam, you score extra points:

500 points if not vulnerable

750 points if vulnerable

A contract of seven (13 tricks) is called a grand slam and if you bid and make a grand slam, you score extra points:

1000 points if not vulnerable

1500 points if vulnerable

If you could make a slam but fail to bid it, you score no extra points and you have missed the opportunity to obtain a large bonus. On the other hand, if you bid a slam and fail to make the tricks required by your contract, you have also lost a valuable score, since you could have made a game.

26 points makes game a good bet, but for a slam you need more points since more tricks are needed. The guidelines are:

With 33 points or more, bid a small slam.

With 37 points or more, bid a grand slam.

If you choose a trump suit, you will want to have at least eight good trumps together, or preferably nine. If unsure, settle for a sure small slam rather than bid a risky grand slam.

Examples

♠ A Q 6   Partner opened 1NT. Your response?
♡ K Q 9   Your 21 points plus partner's 12 at least
◊ A K 5 2   makes 33 or more. Bid 6NT. The maximum
♣ Q J 7   total is 35, not enough to justify 7NT.

♠ A Q J   Partner opened 1NT. Your response?
♡ K J 6   As partner is balanced, you have 9+ clubs
◊ - - -   together. Adding 5 for the void gives you
♣ A J 8 7 6 4 3   21 points and at least 33 together. Bid 6♣.

♠ - - -   Suppose you have opened 1◊ to which
♡ A Q   partner has responded 3◊. What next?
◊ A K 8 6 4 3   As 3◊ shows 4+ support for your suit, you
♣ A 9 6 4 3   can count on at least ten diamonds together.

Adding 5 for your void and 1 for your doubleton, your total point count is 23, and partner's promised 10-12 for 3◊ makes 33 points or more. Your best shot, therefore, is to bid 6◊.

Starting with a two opening

Hands with more than 21 high card points are too strong to open with just a one-opening, since partner may pass such an opening with 0-5 points. Suppose that you hold this hand:

♠ A K 6   If you were to open this with 1♡, imagine
♡ A K 8 7 2   your disappointment if the bidding went No
◊ A K Q J   bid, No bid, No bid. Everyone passing is no
♣ 5   surprise when you have such a powerhouse.

Partner would be quite right to pass with just two or three points, yet that, or even less, could be enough to give you a great chance for game. After three passes, the bidding is over and you would not be permitted to make another bid to increase the contract.

Most hands with 20 points up are too strong for a one-bid. One winner with partner may produce a game, yet partner with just an ace or a king would pass an opening bid of one. To cope with such powerhouses, open with a two-bid. The actual bid depends on the strength and the shape of the hand.

A 2NT opening shows 20-22 points and balanced shape. Partner may pass 2NT with up to 3 points. With any chance for game, partner will respond. If balanced, go for no-trumps. With a long suit, bid three-in-a-suit (a 5-card suit at least and forcing to game) or bid game in a major with a 6+ suit.

Balanced hands with 23 points or more are opened 2♣.

You may also open 2♣ with a powerful hand which is not balanced. 2♣ is an artificial, strong opening bid which shows either 23 HCP up or a hand which contains ten winners or more. You should choose a 2♠, 2♡ or 2♢ opening with around 20-22 HCP and a genuine suit, at least five cards long.

The 2♣ opening: With a weak hand, 7 points or less, responder bids 2♢, an artificial negative reply, saying nothing about diamonds, but merely showing a weak hand. If opener rebids 2NT over 2♢, this is not forcing and shows a balanced hand of 23-24 points. Any other rebid by opener over 2♢ is *forcing to game*. Both partners must keep bidding until a contract of at least 3NT, 4♡, 4♠, 5♣ or 5♢ is reached.

Any response to 2♣ other than 2♢ shows 8 points or better. Bidding continues until the best contract is found and a slam is very likely after such a positive response.

The 2♠, 2♡ and 2♢ openings: Responder must reply to these openings and the negative reply (0-7 points) in each case is 2NT. Any other response shows 8+ points and is forcing to game at least. After a negative 2NT response, if opener repeats the first suit, responder may now pass, but other rebids by opener below game require responder to bid again.

Example hands

(Play hands can be made up by using pages 92-95.)

Hand 13: Dealer North : Both vulnerable

```
                    ♠ 10 9 3 2
                    ♡ K 8 7
                    ◊ 9 8 4
                    ♣ K Q 10
  ♠ 7 6            ┌─────────┐      ♠ A K Q J
  ♡ 10 6 4         │    N    │      ♡ Q 5 3
  ◊ A 10 5 2       │ W     E │      ◊ K Q J
  ♣ J 7 4 2        │    S    │      ♣ A 6 3
                   └─────────┘
                    ♠ 8 5 4
                    ♡ A J 9 2
                    ◊ 7 6 3
                    ♣ 9 8 5
```

RECOMMENDED BIDDING

West	North	East	South
	No	2NT	No
3NT	No	No	No

Bidding: Opposite 20-22, West has enough to raise to 3NT.

Lead: ♡2. Fourth-highest.

Play: North plays the ♡K and returns a heart, giving the defenders the first four tricks. Declarer should win the rest. Be careful not to discard a diamond on the fourth round of hearts. A club discard is safe. Win their switch and overtake the third round of diamonds with dummy's ace, giving declarer four diamonds, four spades and the ace of clubs.

[59]

Hand 14: Dealer East : Nil vulnerable

```
              ♠ 7
              ♡ Q J 7 6 4 3 2
              ◇ 6 4
              ♣ 8 6 5
  ♠ K 9 8 3   ┌─────────┐   ♠ Q 10 6 4
  ♡ 9         │    N    │   ♡ 10 8 5
  ◇ 10 5 3 2  │ W     E │   ◇ K Q J 9
  ♣ K Q J 7   │    S    │   ♣ 10 9
              └─────────┘
              ♠ A J 5 2
              ♡ A K
              ◇ A 8 7
              ♣ A 4 3 2
```

RECOMMENDED BIDDING

West	North	East	South
		No	2NT
No	4♡	All pass	

Bidding: North has enough for game opposite 20-22 but bids 4♡, not 3NT. North knows the partnership has at least nine hearts because the 2NT opening must have at least two hearts. 3NT would be defeated easily.

Lead: ◇K, top of strong sequence.

Play: Win ◇A, play ♡A and ♡K, cash ♠A and ruff a spade. Play ♡Q to draw the last trump and take your other winners. Declarer can make ten tricks via seven heart winners and three outside aces. In no-trumps, South would make just five tricks as South could never reach the winners in the North hand!

[60]

Hand 15: Dealer South : North-South vulnerable

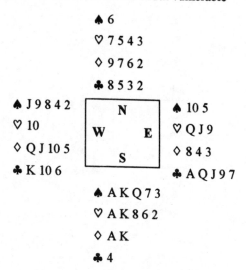

```
                    ♠ 6
                    ♡ 7 5 4 3
                    ◇ 9 7 6 2
                    ♣ 8 5 3 2
    ♠ J 9 8 4 2        ┌─────────┐        ♠ 10 5
    ♡ 10              │    N    │        ♡ Q J 9
    ◇ Q J 10 5       │ W     E │        ◇ 8 4 3
    ♣ K 10 6         │    S    │        ♣ A Q J 9 7
                      └─────────┘
                    ♠ A K Q 7 3
                    ♡ A K 8 6 2
                    ◇ A K
                    ♣ 4
```

RECOMMENDED BIDDING

West	North	East	South
			2♣
No	2◇	No	2♠
No	2NT	No	3♡
No	4♡	All pass	

Bidding: With 23 HCP, South opens 2♣. North must reply, even with no points and 2◇ is the negative reply. South rebids 2♠, forcing to game. With no long suit, North rebids 2NT. 3♡ shows the second suit and North raises to 4♡.

Lead: ◇Q. Top of sequence.

Play: Win ◇A; cash ♡A and ♡K to draw trumps. When they do not divide 2-2, leave the last trump out. Switch to spades and ruff two spade losers in dummy. Making 11 tricks.

```
                    ♠ Q 10 4 2
                    ♡ 5 3
                    ◊ Q 9 7
                    ♣ A K 10 9
♠ A K 9 8 7 6    ┌─────────────┐   ♠ 5 3
♡ A K Q          │      N      │   ♡ 8 7 6 4
◊ A K J          │  W       E  │   ◊ 8 4
♣ 7              │      S      │   ♣ J 8 6 4 3
                 └─────────────┘
                    ♠ J
                    ♡ J 10 9 2
                    ◊ 10 6 5 3 2
                    ♣ Q 5 2
```

RECOMMENDED BIDDING

West	North	East	South
2♣	No	2◊	No
2♠	No	3♣	No
3♠	No	4♠	All pass

Bidding: With such a rockcrusher, West opens 2♣. East bids 2◊, the negative. West shows the spades and East shows the clubs. West rebids the spades to show six (the 2♠ bid already indicated a five-card suit) and this enables East to raise to 4♠.

Lead: ♣A. The standard lead in a trump contract from a suit headed by the A-K is the ace.

Play: West ruffs the second club, cashes ◊A and ◊K, followed by the ◊J, ruffed in dummy. The ace and king of spades are cashed but spades break badly. Making 10 tricks.

Example hands on slam bidding
Hand 17: Dealer North : Nil vulnerable

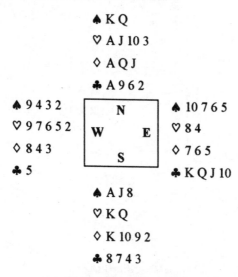

```
                    ♠ K Q
                    ♡ A J 10 3
                    ◊ A Q J
                    ♣ A 9 6 2
    ♠ 9 4 3 2        ┌─────────┐        ♠ 10 7 6 5
    ♡ 9 7 6 5 2      │    N    │        ♡ 8 4
    ◊ 8 4 3      W   │         │   E    ◊ 7 6 5
    ♣ 5             │    S    │        ♣ K Q J 10
                    └─────────┘
                    ♠ A J 8
                    ♡ K Q
                    ◊ K 10 9 2
                    ♣ 8 7 4 3
```

RECOMMENDED BIDDING

West	North	East	South
	2NT	No	6NT
No	No	No	

Bidding: South knows the partnership has 33 points at least and bids the slam. With a balanced hand, South chooses 6NT.

Lead: ♣K. Top of the strong sequence.

Play: There are several ways to make 12 tricks (via 3 spades, 4 hearts, 4 diamonds and 1 club), but declarer must take care not to have winners marooned in dummy or in hand. One way to succeed, after winning the ♣A, is: ♠K, ♠Q overtaken by ♠A, ♠J cashed; ♡K, ♡Q overtaken by ♡A, ♡J and ♡10; ◊A, ◊Q, ◊J overtaken by ◊K and ◊10 cashed. Discard club losers.

Hand 18: Dealer East : North-South vulnerable

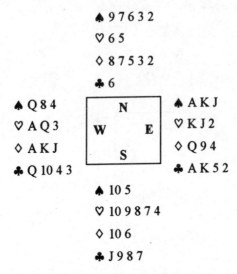

```
                    ♠ 9 7 6 3 2
                    ♡ 6 5
                    ◊ 8 7 5 3 2
                    ♣ 6
    ♠ Q 8 4                         ♠ A K J
    ♡ A Q 3          N              ♡ K J 2
    ◊ A K J       W     E           ◊ Q 9 4
    ♣ Q 10 4 3       S              ♣ A K 5 2
                    ♠ 10 5
                    ♡ 10 9 8 7 4
                    ◊ 10 6
                    ♣ J 9 8 7
```

RECOMMENDED BIDDING

West	North	East	South
		2NT	No
7NT	No	No	No

Bidding: 2NT shows 20-22 points and with 18 points, West counts on 38 points or more, making 7NT a good bet.

Lead: ♡10. Top of sequence.

Play: Even with 39 points, 7NT is no certainty. With 3 spades, 3 hearts and 3 diamonds, declarer needs 4 club tricks. If clubs divide 3-2, there is no problem. To cater for a 4-1 break, declarer must take care to play the ♣A and ♣K first. When North discards on the second club, declarer can capture South's clubs without loss. On the third club, whatever South plays, declarer wins it as cheaply as possible in dummy.

[64]

Hand 19: Dealer South : East-West vulnerable

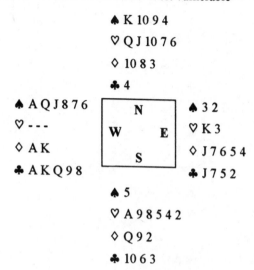

♠ K 10 9 4
♡ Q J 10 7 6
♢ 10 8 3
♣ 4

♠ A Q J 8 7 6
♡ - - -
♢ A K
♣ A K Q 9 8

♠ 3 2
♡ K 3
♢ J 7 6 5 4
♣ J 7 5 2

♠ 5
♡ A 9 8 5 4 2
♢ Q 9 2
♣ 10 6 3

RECOMMENDED BIDDING

West	North	East	South
			No
2♣	No	2♢	No
2♠	No	3♢	No
4♣	No	5♣	No
6♣	No	No	No

Bidding: West's 2♠ shows the longer suit. Over 3♢, West rebids 4♣ to show the second suit. When East raises clubs, West judges that at worst, there might be a spade loser.

Lead: ♡Q. Top of sequence.

Play: Ruff the lead and draw trumps. A spade has to be lost to the king but by ruffing a spade in dummy, West establishes the remaining spades as winners.

[65]

Hand 20: Dealer West : Both vulnerable

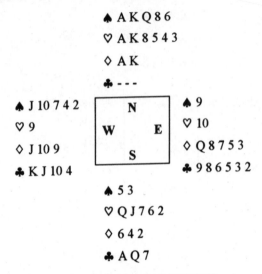

```
              ♠ A K Q 8 6
              ♡ A K 8 5 4 3
              ◇ A K
              ♣ - - -
♠ J 10 7 4 2      N        ♠ 9
♡ 9            W     E      ♡ 10
◇ J 10 9                   ◇ Q 8 7 5 3
♣ K J 10 4        S        ♣ 9 8 6 5 3 2
              ♠ 5 3
              ♡ Q J 7 6 2
              ◇ 6 4 2
              ♣ A Q 7
```

RECOMMENDED BIDDING

West	North	East	South
No	2♣	No	2♡
No	7♡	All pass	

Bidding: North has a huge hand and opens 2♣. South's 2♡ positive response is a most pleasant development for North who sees the partnership must have a magnificent trump fit. As there should be no losers in any suit, North bids 7♡ without ado. (Note that the 7NT grand slam should fail.)

Lead: ◇J. A sequence is safest against a grand slam.

Play: Win ◇A and draw trumps in one round. Then play the top spades. After three rounds, there are still two spades out. Ruff the spade losers in your hand and you have 13 tricks. The ♣A is not even needed!

Chapter 6

OTHER ASPECTS OF BIDDING

The preceding chapters cover the essentials and allow you to play bridge in a just a few hours. Here are some other bidding techniques which you may encounter and which you will need to learn in the subsequent development of your skills.

Opening bids of three and four

Opening bids at the three-level or four-level are *weak* openings based on a long, strong suit (at least a seven-card suit). The strength is below 11 HCP. The opening bids of 5♣ and 5♦ are also weak, with an eight- or nine-card suit. The 3NT opening shows a 7-card or longer minor suit headed by the A-K-Q.

These are called 'pre-emptive' openings because their aim is to shut out the opposition. A pre-empt should be within three tricks of the bid not vulnerable and two tricks if vulnerable.

Overcalls and jump-overcalls

There is only one opening bid in each auction, the first bid. The side that does not open is called the 'defending' side and a suit or a no-trump bid by the defenders is an 'overcall'.

The 1NT overcall shows 16-18 points, balanced shape and a stopper in the enemy suit. A stopper is a high card which can prevent the opponents from cashing a suit from the top. The ace, K-x, Q-x-x or J-x-x-x is the minimum requirement for a stopper. ('x' is any card below a ten, a worthless card, a 'rag'.) The 1NT overcall is stronger than opening 1NT, but overcalls in a suit may have fewer HCP than an opening bid in a suit.

A suit overcall does not require 12 points. You may overcall with considerably less than that. What is needed is a strong five-card or longer suit, normally with two or three top honours. At the one-level, a suit overcall shows 8-15 HCP and a strong five-card suit. At the two-level, the range is 10-15 HCP and a strong five-card suit. The powerful suit is essential.

A jump-overcall in a suit shows a good six-card or longer suit and about 16-19 HCP. It is not a forcing bid but it encourages partner to try for a game.

A pre-emptive overcall is a jump-overcall which skips two or more levels, e.g., (1♡) : 3♠ or (1♡) : 4♣. It is a weak bid, based on about 6-10 HCP and a seven- or eight-card suit.

Penalty doubles vs. takeout doubles

At your turn to bid you may double a bid by an opponent. You simply say 'Double'. The primary aim of a double is to increase the penalties when the opponents fail in their contract. A bid following a double cancels the double (as it cancels any other bid) but does not prevent a subsequent double. You may redouble only a double by an opponent. This aims to increase the scoring further (see the Scoring Table, page 96). There is no re-redouble or re-re-redouble.

When a double is meant for penalties, partner is requested to pass. A double is for penalties in standard methods when it occurs at the three-level or higher or when it is a double of a bid of no-trumps or if it occurs after partner has made a bid.

Another kind of double exists, the 'takeout double'. This is a request for partner to bid, to take out the double, remove it by making a bid. A double is for takeout if it is a double of a suit bid at the one-level or two-level and partner has not yet made a bid. It is vital to recognise the difference between the two types of double since the penalty double asks you to pass and the takeout double asks you to bid.

A takeout double should have about the equivalent strength of an opening bid. With minimum values, the doubler should be short in the opponents' suit and should have three-card or four-card support for the unbid suits. The takeout double is forcing and with a very weak hand, partner bids a suit (0-9 points) or 1NT (6-9 points).

The Blackwood Convention

'Blackwood' is a bid of 4NT which asks partner, 'How many aces do you have?'. There are four possible answers:

$$5\clubsuit = 0 \text{ or } 4 \text{ aces}$$
$$5\diamond = 1 \text{ ace}$$
$$5\heartsuit = 2 \text{ aces}$$
$$5\spadesuit = 3 \text{ aces}$$

After the answer to 4NT, a bid of 5NT asks for kings, and the answers follow a similar pattern ($6\clubsuit$ = no king, $6\diamond$ = 1, $6\heartsuit$ = 2, $6\spadesuit$ = 3 and 6NT = 4 kings). 4NT to ask for aces is used when you know you have enough points for a slam and you also know which suit is going to be trumps. The 4NT bidder makes the decision as to the final contract. The 5NT ask for kings is used if you have enough to try for a grand slam and the partnership is known to hold all the aces.

The Stayman 2♣ convention

After an opening bid of 1NT, a response of 2♣ is used as a question: 'Do you have a four-card major suit?' The answers:

$$2\diamond = \text{No major suit}$$
$$2\heartsuit = \text{I have four hearts}$$
$$2\spadesuit = \text{I have four spades}$$

With both majors, show the hearts first.

Use the Stayman 2♣ convention when you hold at least one four-card major and eleven or more points. 2NT : 3♣ is used the same way with at least one major and four or more points.

Chapter 7

TIPS ON DECLARER PLAY

FOR NO-TRUMPS

1. Count your instant winners.

2. Decide which suit will provide the extra tricks needed.

3. Play that suit and do not worry about giving up the lead.

4. Set up the extra tricks first, cash your sure winners later.

FOR TRUMP CONTRACTS

1. Count your losers, suit by suit, based on your own hand.

2. See which losers are covered by winning cards in dummy.

3. If you have too many losers, check whether you can ruff losers in dummy or discard them on extra winners in dummy.

4. It is normally sensible to draw trumps early. However, do not draw trumps straight away if you need a quick discard or if you need dummy's trumps to ruff your losers.

5. Prefer to trump losers in the shorter trump hand. You rarely gain a trick by trumping in the long trump hand.

6. If there is one trump out, draw it if it is lower than yours but if it is higher than yours, it is often best to leave it out and tackle the other suits.

The hold-up play

In no-trumps, if you hold A-x-x and dummy has x-x or x-x-x, you should normally hold off with your ace until the third round, unless some other suit is even more dangerous. The hold-up play is rarely necessary in a trump contract.

High-card-from-shortage

Where you have winners in both hands, play the winners first from the hand with fewer cards (the short hand). For example, if dummy has two cards and you have three, play dummy's winners first. This enables you to take all the tricks to which you are entitled and will prevent suits being blocked.

DECLARER	DUMMY	Play the jack and the two on
A-K-Q-2	J-5	the first round.

   The same principle applies when knocking out an ace:

DECLARER	DUMMY	Play the king first and the
K-Q-4	J-10-5-2	queen on the second round.

Count the missing cards

All good players keep track of the cards that are missing in each suit. This is a tough task when you are just learning but with practice you will become quite proficient at it. Start by counting just the missing cards in the trump suit or in your longest suit in no-trumps. Once you have mastered that, you can extend your skill to the next longest suit and before long, you will be able to do it in all four suits.

   The best way to count the cards is to work out as soon as dummy appears how many cards the opponents hold in the critical suit. If you and dummy have 8, they have 5; if you and dummy have 9, they have 4, and so on. Then you simply concentrate on the cards they play and deduct that each time. With practice, this will become second nature to you.

Chapter 8

TIPS ON DEFENDING

Opening leads against no-trumps
Lead your long suit against no-trumps unless partner has bid a suit (prefer to lead partner's suit) or the opponents have bid your long suit (prefer to lead some other suit). The card to lead in your long suit is the top card from a three-card or longer sequence (the Q from Q-J-10-5-2), but when you do not have a sequence, lead fourth highest (the 5 from K-J-7-5-2).

Opening leads against trump contracts
The long suit is no longer so appealing since the opponents may be able to ruff on the second or third round of the suit. A short suit lead is usually more appealing as you will be able to ruff as soon as you become void. If partner has bid a suit, prefer to lead that suit. If partner has not bid, avoid leading a suit bid by the opposition. The best leads are suits headed by a three-card sequence, a suit headed by A-K or a singleton lead.

Leads to avoid are suits headed by the ace without the king, doubleton honours such as K-x, Q-x or J-x when partner has not bid the suit, or singleton trump leads.

The card to lead from a long suit is the same as in no-trumps, top from a three-card or longer sequence or fourth-highest when you do not hold such a sequence, but there are three exceptions to this approach:

1. From A-K-x-x or longer, lead the fourth-highest against no-trumps, but lead the ace against a suit contract.

2. From K-Q-x-x or longer, lead the fourth-highest against no-trumps, but lead the king against a suit contract.

3. From A-x-x-x or longer, lead the fourth-highest against no-trumps. Against suit contracts, try to avoid leading a suit headed by the ace unless you have the king as well, but if you must lead the suit, lead the ace, not a low one.

When leading a short suit:

1. Lead top card from a doubleton (the 8 from 8-6).

2. From a tripleton, lead the top card from a three-card or two-card sequence headed by an honour (the Q from Q-J-5), lead the bottom card when you hold an honour card or two honours not in sequence (the 5 from Q-9-5) and lead the middle card when you hold no honour card (the 7 from 8-7-3).

Defence after the opening lead

It is often best to play second-hand-low and third-hand-high, but these rules need to be tempered to the situation. It is normal to return your partner's lead, but be prepared to switch to another suit if your suit is very strong or if returning partner's suit is clearly futile. It is generally not a good idea to lead a suit which dummy can trump. 'Cover an honour with an honour' is good advice only if this would build up a trick for your side.

Higher-card-then-lower in third seat or when discarding is a signal asking partner to continue playing that suit. Lowest card in third seat (or discard of lowest card) asks partner to discontinue that suit and switch to some other suit.

Example hands on defending

(Play hands can be made up by using pages 92-95.)

Hand 21: Dealer North : North-South vulnerable

```
                    ♠ A K 8
                    ♡ 9 8 7
                    ◇ A 8 4 3
                    ♣ K 8 3
    ♠ 10 9 3 2    ┌─────────┐    ♠ 7 5 4
    ♡ A 6         │    N    │    ♡ K Q J 3 2
    ◇ 9 7 5       │ W     E │    ◇ 10 6
    ♣ 10 6 4 2    │    S    │    ♣ J 9 7
                  └─────────┘
                    ♠ Q J 6
                    ♡ 10 5 4
                    ◇ K Q J 2
                    ♣ A Q 5
```

RECOMMENDED BIDDING

West	North	East	South
	1NT	No	3NT
No	No	No	

Bidding: A routine 1NT : 3NT auction.

Lead: ♡K. Top of sequence.

Play: West should overtake the ♡K lead with the ace and return the ♡6. East wins and continues hearts. The defence takes the first five tricks. If West plays low at trick one, declarer makes ten tricks. West should recognise from the *king* lead that East has K-Q-J and thus by playing low in hearts, only two tricks will be taken; by overtaking you can take more.

[74]

Hand 22: Dealer East : East-West vulnerable

```
                    ♠ J 10 4
                    ♡ 9 2
                    ◊ 9 2
                    ♣ A 8 7 6 3 2
♠ A K Q 9      ┌─────────┐      ♠ 8 3 2
♡ K 5 4        │    N    │      ♡ A Q J 8 7 6
◊ J 8 7 6      │  W   E  │      ◊ K 10 3
♣ 5 4          │    S    │      ♣ K
               └─────────┘
                    ♠ 7 6 5
                    ♡ 10 3
                    ◊ A Q 5 4
                    ♣ Q J 10 9
```

RECOMMENDED BIDDING

West	North	East	South
		1♡	No
1♠	No	2♡	No
4♡	No	No	No

Bidding: West bids 1♠, up-the-line with four-card suits.

Lead: ♣Q. Top of sequence.

Play: North should play the ♣A since the ♣Q denies the king. When East's ♣K falls, North should realise that declarer has no more clubs amd would ruff a club continuation. It is also clear by looking at dummy that a spade switch would be futile. Therefore, shift to the *nine* of diamonds (top from a doubleton) and after South wins two diamonds, a third diamond can be ruffed by North to defeat the contract.

[75]

Hand 23: Dealer South : Both vulnerable

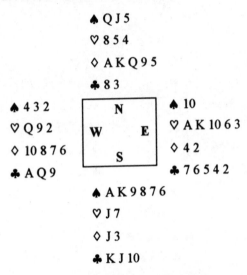

```
                    ♠ Q J 5
                    ♡ 8 5 4
                    ◊ A K Q 9 5
                    ♣ 8 3
    ♠ 4 3 2                          ♠ 10
    ♡ Q 9 2          N               ♡ A K 10 6 3
    ◊ 10 8 7 6    W     E            ◊ 4 2
    ♣ A Q 9          S               ♣ 7 6 5 4 2
                    ♠ A K 9 8 7 6
                    ♡ J 7
                    ◊ J 3
                    ♣ K J 10
```

RECOMMENDED BIDDING

West	North	East	South
			1♠
No	2◊	No	2♠
No	4♠	All pass	

Bidding: Natural and sensible.

Lead: ♡2, bottom from three to an honour. Do not lead a diamond (dummy's suit) or a club (ace but no king). On a diamond, South makes 11 tricks and at least 10 on ♣A lead.

Play: After two hearts, East realises from West's ♡2-9 that West has the last heart. With 9-2 doubleton, play 9 first, 2 next. High-low shows a doubleton. As declarer would ruff the next heart, East switches to ♣4 and the defenders take the first four tricks. If East plays a third heart, South can make 11 tricks

Hand 24: Dealer West : Nil vulnerable

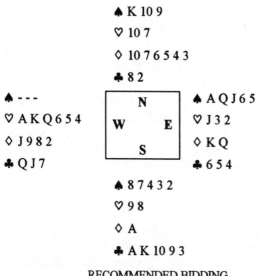

```
                    ♠ K 10 9
                    ♡ 10 7
                    ◊ 10 7 6 5 4 3
                    ♣ 8 2
    ♠ - - -              N           ♠ A Q J 6 5
    ♡ A K Q 6 5 4    W       E       ♡ J 3 2
    ◊ J 9 8 2            S           ◊ K Q
    ♣ Q J 7                          ♣ 6 5 4
                    ♠ 8 7 4 3 2
                    ♡ 9 8
                    ◊ A
                    ♣ A K 10 9 3
```

RECOMMENDED BIDDING

West	North	East	South
1♡	No	1♠	2♣
2♡	No	4♡	All pass

Bidding: South's suit is strong enough to overcall. West could rebid 2◊ but the hearts are so much stronger and longer.

Lead: ♣8, top from a doubleton. Even without South's bid, the doubleton club is appealing. The weaker the hand, the more attractive is a short suit lead since partner figures to have entries to give you ruffs. A spade lead gives West 11 tricks.

Play: After ♣K-A, South can play a third club for North to ruff. This puts 4♡ one down, but South can do even better: win the top clubs, cash ◊A (create your own void), then give North a club ruff and receive a diamond ruff to beat 4♡ by two tricks.

Chapter 9

THE WORLD OF BRIDGE

There are two different forms of contract bridge. Rubber bridge (or social bridge) is played mainly in private homes and in a few clubs. The aim is to win rubbers and the scoring is according to the table on page 96. The most important feature is that your score on each deal is carried forward to the next deal until the rubber is concluded.

Duplicate bridge (or competitive bridge) is played mainly in bridge clubs. Each deal is independent and you are rewarded when you make a part-score or a game by extra bonuses (50 for a part-score, 300 for a game not vulnerable, 500 for a game vulnerable). Honours do not count. A duplicate game has a 'director', who has a number of functions, including organising the game, ruling on any infractions and scoring the results.

At the start of a duplicate session, the cards are shuffled and dealt, but thereafter there is no more shuffling and dealing. You play your cards in front of you (not into the middle of the table) and at the end of each deal, you return your thirteen cards to the correct position in the 'board' (card container). This allows other pairs to play exactly the same deals as you have played. You play against different opponents on each round which normally consists of two or three deals. After each round, you meet new opponents and the boards are moved to new tables.

There are two main types of duplicate tournaments, pairs events and teams events. An individual tournament is held occasionally (usually no more than once a year in each club or county) where you change partners, opponents and boards after each round. At club level, most events are pairs games where you play with the same partner throughout the event. At county and national level, the division between pairs and teams games is roughly even and at international level, most events are contested by teams, representing their country.

In a teams event, you compete against one other team at a time. A team consists of four, five or six players but only four members play at any one time. At one table Team A sits North-South while Team B sits East-West. After a board is completed, it goes to the other table where the other Team A pair sits East-West and the other pair from Team B sits North-South. There is thus a direct comparison between the results obtained by each team on each deal. This is the fairest kind of tournament since your score is not affected by any results other than your own and the luck factor is eliminated.

The World Bridge Federation was formed in 1958 and has over 100 members. The WBF organises world championships each year, teams events every year and pairs events every four years. The major world championships are the open teams (the Bermuda Bowl), the women's teams (the Venice trophy), the Junior Teams (for players under 26 years of age) and the World Teams Olympiad (open and women's teams) in Olympic years. From 1957 to 1975 Italy dominated the world championships but since then many countries have been successful including Brazil, France, Germany, Great Britain, Iceland, the Netherlands, Poland and the United States. The USA has more top class players than any other country.

WHERE TO NEXT?

You should start playing as soon as possible, preferably with a group of friends of about the same standard. If you can arrange supervision by a good, sympathetic player, so much the better.

Do not be discouraged if you find some early difficulty in remembering all the rules and the number of points needed for various bids. With a little practice, they will become second nature to you. After playing a few games, it will be worthwhile to read this book carefully again. Some of the points you may have forgotten will be refreshed and other points may now make more sense. After some more games, another reading will not go amiss. A handy quick-reference flipper guide which you will find useful is the *Basic Acol Bridge Flipper*.

After playing for two to six months, you will be ready for a more comprehensive textbook. Recommended is *Basic Bridge* which covers all the standard material you will need at this early stage. It also has an accompanying reference guide, the *Acol Bridge Flipper*. There are many other good bridge books. At this stage, concentrate on those dealing with card play.

As most towns have bridge clubs, you should be able to find a club reasonably handy. Once you can play at the standard of this book, do consider joining a bridge club if you wish to improve your game. If available, a large bridge club is best since it will provide classes conducted by a competent teacher, play sessions supervised by a good teacher or player, and special sessions for novice players only. Supervised play sessions are excellent while you are still learning.

It is best not to play against very strong players until you have had a fair amount of experience. Their methods may confuse you and strong players tend to play much too quickly for novices, making it harder to follow what is going on and not giving you enough time to work out your best play. If you feel timid about playing in experienced company, you can still learn a good deal by watching strong players in action. Do not say anything during the game. Concentrate on just one player's cards and try to decide what you would bid or play before the player makes that decision and see whether your bids or plays match the player's. After a hand is over, most good players do not mind if you ask them a question or two.

If asked to have a game, do not refuse but explain that you are still a novice. If you are lucky, you may have a partner who is better than you and can point out your mistakes kindly. Try to find another enthusiastic player of about your own standard so that you can compete together in the club events, discuss what happens at the tournaments and improve together.

If you are a schoolboy or schoolgirl, find out whether your school has a bridge club. If not, you might find other students with whom you could start a school club. There are some inter-school competitions but do not become overzealous with your bridge. Your schoolwork is still more important, but you can combine it with a healthy interest in bridge.

Appendix

THE MECHANICS AND RULES OF
BRIDGE — HOW THE GAME IS PLAYED

This section will help to dispel any doubts you might have about the rules or technicalities when playing bridge.

Bridge is a game for four players, playing in two partnerships. Partners sit opposite each other. Partnerships are chosen by agreement or by lot. The most common method is for each player to choose a card from the pack fanned out face down, with the players selecting the two highest cards as one partnership against the players selecting the two lowest cards. After a rubber has ended, new partnerships may be selected.

The bridge pack

A regular pack of 52 cards is used. There are no jokers and no cards of any exceptional rank or function. There are four suits:

♠ SPADES   ♥ HEARTS   ♦ DIAMONDS   ♣ CLUBS

Each suit contains thirteen cards which in order of rank are: A, K, Q, J, 10, 9, 8, 7, 6, 5, 4, 3, 2. An ace beats a king, a king beats a queen, a queen beats a jack, and so on. The top five cards in each suit, the A, K, Q, J and 10, are known as the honour cards or honours.

The suits also have a ranking order: Clubs (♣) is the *lowest* suit, then come Diamonds (♦) and Hearts (♥) to the highest ranking suit, Spades (♠). No-trumps ranks higher than any suit. The order of the suits — C, D, H, S, — is no accident. They are in alphabetical order.

When selecting partnerships, if two cards of the same rank are chosen, the tie is broken if necessary by suit order.

Dealing

The person who drew the highest card is the first dealer and has the right to choose seats and the pack of cards with which to deal. The next dealer will be the person on the left of the previous dealer and so on, in clockwise rotation. The cards are shuffled by the player on dealer's left. The dealer passes the pack to the player on dealer's right to be cut. The dealer then deals the cards, one at a time, face down, clockwise, starting with the player on the left, until all 52 cards are dealt, 13 each

It is courteous to leave the cards face down until they have all been dealt. A misdeal may be corrected if the players have not seen the cards. As the cards are dealt, the partner of the dealer shuffles the other pack and places the shuffled pack face down on the shuffler's right, ready for the next dealer to pick up. Two packs are used in order to speed up the game.

The start of play

When you pick up your 13 cards, sort them into suits. It is normal to separate the red suits and black suits.

After the bidding ends, the side that bid higher wins the right to play the hand. The member of this side who bid the trump suit (or no-trumps) first, is the 'declarer'. Declarer plays the hand while the opponents 'defend' the hand. The player on the left of declarer places a card face up on the table (the opening 'lead'). Declarer's partner, the 'dummy', now puts all thirteen cards face up on the table and arranged in suits. The dummy takes no further part in the play, declarer playing both hands.

After the opening lead, declarer plays one of the cards from dummy, then the third player plays a card and declarer plays a card from hand. The four cards now face up on the table are called a 'trick'. A trick always consists of four cards played in clockwise sequence, one from each hand.

[83]

A trick is won by the highest card played. The player who wins the trick gathers the four cards together, puts them face down neatly and then leads to the next trick, and so on until all thirteen tricks have been played. (In tournament bridge, called 'duplicate', the cards are not gathered together. The players keep their own cards in front of them.) Each deal is a battle over thirteen tricks, declarer trying to win the number of tricks nominated in the bidding, or more, while the defenders try to win enough tricks to defeat declarer.

Following suit

The player who plays the highest ranking card *of the suit led* wins the trick. What if two or more cards of the same rank are played to one trick, who wins then? The basic rule of play is: *you must follow suit*, i.e., you must play a card of the same suit as the suit led. If hearts are led, then you must play a heart if you have one and the trick is won by the highest heart played. If unable to follow suit, you may play any other card at all, but remember it is the highest card of the suit led which wins. If the king of spades is led, it will do you no good to play the ace of clubs. Only the ace of spades beats the king of spades.

Trumps

There is one exception to this. Where one of the four suits is made the *trump* suit in the bidding, any card in the trump suit is higher than any card, even an ace, in one of the other suits. So if hearts are trumps, the two of hearts would beat the ace of clubs even when clubs are led. But, first and foremost, you must follow suit. To play a trump card to beat a high card of another suit, you must have no cards in the suit led.

If unable to follow suit, you may trump in, *but it is not obligatory*. You may choose to discard. If partner has already won the trick, it may be foolish to trump partner's winner.

A trick with no trump card is won by the highest card in the suit led, otherwise by the highest trump. If you fail to follow suit when able to do so, you have 'revoked' (or 'reneged'). The penalty for a revoke is to transfer one or two tricks to the other side, usually one trick if you do not win the revoking trick, two tricks if you do win the revoking trick.

The bidding

The play is preceded by the bidding, also called 'the auction'. In the bridge auction each side tries to outbid the other for the right to be declarer and play the hand.

The dealer makes the first bid, then the player on dealer's left and so on in clockwise rotation. Each player may pass (say 'No Bid') or make a bid. A player who has previously passed may still bid later in the auction. A bid consists of a number (1, 2, 3, 4, 5, 6 or 7) followed by a suit or no-trumps, for example, three hearts, two diamonds, four no-trumps, seven diamonds. 'No-trumps' means there is to be no trump suit on the deal.

A bid indicates the number of tricks *above six* to be won in the play. The minimum number of tricks you may contract for is seven (just above half of the thirteen tricks). A bid of 1 Club contracts to make at least seven tricks with clubs as trumps. The number in the bid is the number of tricks to be won *over and above six tricks*. The final bid is the 'contract'.

If all players pass without a bid on the first round, there is no play, there is no score, the cards are thrown in and the next dealer deals a new hand. After the first bid, the auction has started and will be won by the side that bids higher. Bidding continues, with each player bidding or passing, until a bid is followed by three passes. The final bid sets the trump suit (or no-trumps) and the number of tricks to be won in the play. The member of the side who first bid the trump suit (or no-trumps) becomes the declarer.

After a bid, any player in turn may make a *higher* bid. A bid is higher if the number is larger, or the number is the same but the denomination is higher ranking. The order is No-trumps (highest), Spades, Hearts, Diamonds, down to Clubs (lowest).

A bid of 1 Heart is higher than a bid of 1 Club. To bid Clubs if the previous bid was 2 Spades, you need to bid 3 Clubs.

Game and rubber

A rubber of bridge is over when one side wins two games. A game is won by scoring 100 or more points when declarer.

The scoring is important because it affects the strategy in both the bidding and the play. Your aim is to score more points than the opposition. You may score points: (1) by bidding and making a contract as declarer, (2) by defeating the opponents at their contract, or (3) by earning bonus points.

Some points are written above the line, some below the line on the scoresheet. When adding up the totals at the end of the rubber, all points count equally, but points below the line are valuable during the rubber, since these are the only points that count towards game. *Only the declarer side can score points for game.* That is the incentive for bidding higher than the opponents. You score points below the line by bidding and making a contract, according to this table:

No-Trumps (NT)	30 points for each trick over six, plus 10
♠ SPADES	30 points for each trick over six
♡ HEARTS	30 points for each trick over six
◊ DIAMONDS	20 points for each trick over six
♣ CLUBS	20 points for each trick over six

As game is 100 points or more, it requires a bid of 5 Clubs or 5 Diamonds to make game in the minors. A bid of 4 Hearts or 4 Spades will score game in the majors. In no-trumps, it takes a bid of only 3NT to score a game.

If declarer makes the tricks required, or more, the declaring side gets credit below the line for the number of tricks in the contract and above the line for the extras (the overtricks). If declarer fails, the opponents score points, depending on the number of tricks by which declarer failed.

Only points scored by winning the actual number of tricks in the contract are written below the line and only points below the line count towards winning games and the rubber.

It is accuracy in bidding that distinguishes contract bridge from auction bridge where you are given credit for what you make, even if you did not bid it.

A score below the line of less than 100 is a 'part-score'. You may combine two or more part-scores to score the 100 points for game. You cannot carry forward any points beyond 100 to the next game. After one side scores a game, a line is drawn across both columns and both sides start the next game from zero. So, if you have a part-score but the enemy score a game before you have been able to convert your part-score into a game, you have to start again from zero.

Doubles and redoubles
In the bidding, any player may, at his turn, double a bid made by an opponent. Say 'Double'. If there is no further bidding, the double increases the rewards for success and the penalties for failure. After a double, the other side may redouble (say 'Redouble'), increasing the rewards and penalties further.

Any double or redouble is cancelled by a bid, but there may be further doubles and redoubles of later bids. 1 Spade doubled and redoubled making 7 tricks scores 120 below the line (and game!), plus 100 bonus points above the line for making a doubled contract ('for the insult').

Other scoring

There is a complete scoring table on page 96 to which you can refer if in doubt. You *should know the trick value of each suit and no-trumps* (see page 86), and you should also know some of the more common scores which go above the line, but the rest of the scoring can be learned gradually, as you play.

Upon winning one game, a side is 'vulnerable'. Penalties are more severe for failing to make a contract when vulnerable than when not vulnerable.

When one side fails to make its contract, the other side scores points above the line as follows:

The declarer side is not vulnerable: 50 points per undertrick.

The declarer side is vulnerable: 100 points per undertrick.

If the final contract is doubled or redoubled, the penalties are more severe (see the scoring table, page 96). Note that penalties are the same regardless of the contract. One down in 2 Clubs is the same score as one down in 7 No-trumps.

You may score bonus points for finishing the rubber. If you end the rubber, you score above the line:

700 points if the opponents are not vulnerable (2 games to 0).

500 points if the opponents are vulnerable (2 games to 1).

You score bonus points for making overtricks in a doubled or redoubled contract (see scoring table) and also for being lucky enough to hold good cards, for holding 'honours'. The honour cards are the A, K, Q, J and 10. You score above the line:

150 for all 5 trump honours in one hand.

100 for any 4 of the 5 trump honours in one hand.

150 for 4 aces in one hand, but only if the contract is NT.

The bonus for honours is scored whether or not the contract is made. Honours may be held by declarer, dummy or either defender. Honours are usually claimed after the hand has been played. Honours are not scored at duplicate.

A contract of six (12 tricks) is called a small slam and if you *bid and make* a small slam, you score above the line:

500 points if not vulnerable

750 points if vulnerable.

A contract of seven (13 tricks) is called a grand slam, and if you *bid and make* a grand slam, you score above the line:

1000 points if not vulnerable

1500 points if vulnerable.

The score for the rubber is entered next to each player's name on a tally card and the next rubber is then started, either with the same partnerships or by drawing again for new partners. Bridge may be played without stakes or with stakes. The amount of the stakes is by agreement among the players before play commences and is usually stipulated at so much per hundred points, e.g., 10p per hundred, £1 per hundred.

The aim of the game

The aim in bridge is to score more points than the opponents. If the partnership hands can produce a game (or a slam) and game (slam) is not bid, a valuable score has been lost. The rewards for success at game-level outweigh the loss for failure.

If the opposition can bid and make a game or a slam, you are better off to bid higher than the opponents and fail, provided that the penalty for defeat is less than the value of their contract. Accept a small loss (a 'sacrifice') rather than let the opposition score a game or a slam.

You need not succeed in every game you bid. The rewards for finishing a rubber are so great that failing now and again is no tragedy and a failure rate in games of 1 in 4 is normal and expected. Suppose that you bid 3NT four times and fail on two occasions but succeed on two occasions. Your success rate is only 50% but you are some 700 points in front. The moral is: Do not fret if you do not make every contract you bid.

A comparison of two rubbers

(A)			(B)	
WE	THEY		WE	THEY
700 (2)			700 (2)	
90 (2)			750 (2)	
20 (1)			500 (1)	
100 (1)			120 (1)	
100 (2)			190 (2)	

A: (1) 5♣, 12 tricks   (2) 3NT, 12 tricks   Total: 1010, (+10)
B: (1) 6♣, 12 tricks   (2) 6NT, 12 tricks   Total: 2260, (+23)

Note that the tricks taken were the same for each pair but Pair B won more than twice as much as Pair A because Pair B bid their slams and won 500 and 750 extra bonus points. If you fail to bid an available slam, you have missed a large bonus.

Bridge behaviour and ethics

Bridge has a code of laws which includes a section on the proprieties which deals with proper behaviour at the bridge table. Table talk (anything other than the legal bids) is not welcome in a serious game. In particular, it is the height of rudeness to criticise partner or the opponents. You should be on your best behaviour at the bridge table at all times and a friendly, cheerful disposition will make you a welcome addition to any game. Above all, bridge is meant to be fun.

Play Hands

Play Hands for NORTH (* = dealer)

1*	2	3	4
♠ 10 6 4 3	♠ K 8 4 2	♠ A J 8	♠ K 8 2
♡ Q 10 7 5 2	♡ 10 5	♡ A K 2	♡ K Q 3
◊ 10	◊ K 10 7	◊ 7 3 2	◊ 9 6 4 3
♣ K Q 9	♣ J 5 3 2	♣ Q J 8 2	♣ 7 6 4

5*	6	7	8
♠ A K 8 6 4 3	♠ 7 2	♠ 2	♠ J 6 4 2
♡ A J 2	♡ K J 9 8	♡ Q 9 3	♡ A K Q
◊ K Q 3	◊ Q 7 5 3	◊ 9 8 7 5	◊ 9 8 3
♣ 7	♣ 9 8 6	♣ A K 5 4 3	♣ 9 8 6

9*	10	11	12
♠ K Q J 5 4 2	♠ 10 5 4	♠ K 5 2	♠ 10 2
♡ A 8 3	♡ 10	♡ K 9	♡ Q 9 6 4
◊ 7	◊ K Q J 6	◊ A 7 5 4	◊ A 10 9 7 6
♣ Q J 5	♣ K 9 8 6 2	♣ J 9 4 3	♣ J 10

13*	14	15	16
♠ 10 9 3 2	♠ 7	♠ 6	♠ Q 10 4 2
♡ K 8 7	♡ Q J 7 6 4 3 2	♡ 7 5 4 3	♡ 5 3
◊ 9 8 4	◊ 6 4	◊ 9 7 6 2	◊ Q 9 7
♣ K Q 10	♣ 8 6 5	♣ 8 5 3 2	♣ A K 10 9

17*	18	19	20
♠ K Q	♠ 9 7 6 3 2	♠ K 10 9 4	♠ A K Q 8 6
♡ A J 10 3	♡ 6 5	♡ Q J 10 7 6	♡ A K 8 5 4 3
◊ A Q J	◊ 8 7 5 3 2	◊ 10 8 3	◊ A K
♣ A 9 6 2	♣ 6	♣ 4	♣ - - -

21*	22	23	24
♠ A K 8	♠ J 10 4	♠ Q J 5	♠ K 10 9
♡ 9 8 7	♡ 9 2	♡ 8 5 4	♡ 10 7
◊ A 8 4 3	◊ 9 2	◊ A K Q 9 5	◊ 10 7 6 5 4 3
♣ K 8 3	♣ A 8 7 6 3 2	♣ 8 3	♣ 8 2

Play Hands for EAST (* = dealer)

1
♠ K 8 5
♡ A 6
♦ K Q 8 6 4
♣ 7 6 4

2*
♠ J 10 9 5
♡ 4 3
♦ J 6 5
♣ Q 7 6 4

3
♠ K 6
♡ 10 9 8 6 3
♦ A 10 8 5 4
♣ 6

4
♠ 9 5
♡ 10 9 7 2
♦ A K Q
♣ 10 5 3 2

5
♠ J
♡ K 10 4 3
♦ 10 8 7 4
♣ Q J 10 9

6*
♠ J 10
♡ 6 4 2
♦ A K J 10
♣ J 10 7 3

7
♠ J 8 6 5 4
♡ J
♦ K 4 3 2
♣ Q 7 6

8
♠ K 9 5 3
♡ 8 4 3
♦ K 5 4
♣ Q 7 2

9
♠ 9
♡ Q J 10 7 5
♦ 9 3 2
♣ 10 8 7 3

10*
♠ K Q 8 3 2
♡ A J 9 6
♦ 7
♣ A 5 4

11
♠ Q 7 6
♡ J 10 8 6
♦ 10
♣ A 10 8 6 2

12
♠ A Q 7 6
♡ A J 3
♦ 8 4 2
♣ K 8 6

13
♠ A K Q J
♡ Q 5 3
♦ K Q J
♣ A 6 3

14*
♠ Q 10 6 4
♡ 10 8 5
♦ K Q J 9
♣ 10 9

15
♠ 10 5
♡ Q J 9
♦ 8 4 3
♣ A Q J 9 7

16
♠ 5 3
♡ 8 7 6 4
♦ 8 4
♣ J 8 6 4 3

17
♠ 10 7 6 5
♡ 8 4
♦ 7 6 5
♣ K Q J 10

18*
♠ A K J
♡ K J 2
♦ Q 9 4
♣ A K 5 2

19
♠ 3 2
♡ K 3
♦ J 7 6 5 4
♣ J 7 5 2

20
♠ 9
♡ 10
♦ Q 8 7 5 3
♣ 9 8 6 5 3 2

21
♠ 7 5 4
♡ K Q J 3 2
♦ 10 6
♣ J 9 7

22*
♠ 8 3 2
♡ A Q J 8 7 6
♦ K 10 3
♣ K

23
♠ 10
♡ A K 10 6 3
♦ 4 2
♣ 7 6 5 4 2

24
♠ A Q J 6 5
♡ J 3 2
♦ K Q
♣ 6 5 4

Play Hands for SOUTH (* = dealer)

1
♠ J 9 7
♡ J 8 4
♢ 9 5 3
♣ A 10 8 2

2
♠ Q 7 6
♡ Q J 9 2
♢ Q 9
♣ A 10 9 8

3*
♠ 7 5 4 2
♡ Q J
♢ K Q J 6
♣ A K 4

4
♠ A 6 3
♡ A 5 4
♢ 10 8 7 5
♣ K Q J

5
♠ Q 9 5 2
♡ 7
♢ J 6 5 2
♣ K 8 5 4

6
♠ A K 9 6 4
♡ A Q 10 3
♢ 6
♣ 5 4 2

7*
♠ K Q 10
♡ K 10 4
♢ 10 6
♣ J 10 9 8 2

8
♠ Q 10 8
♡ J 10 9 6 2
♢ J 7
♣ A 5 4

9
♠ A 7 3
♡ 6
♢ K Q 8 5 4
♣ A 6 4 2

10
♠ A J 7 6
♡ 8 7 2
♢ 10 9 8 3
♣ J 10

11*
♠ A 4 3
♡ A Q 7 5 4 3
♢ K Q 6
♣ 7

12
♠ J 9 8
♡ 10 8 7 5
♢ K Q J
♣ 9 5 4

13
♠ 8 5 4
♡ A J 9 2
♢ 7 6 3
♣ 9 8 5

14
♠ A J 5 2
♡ A K
♢ A 8 7
♣ A 4 3 2

15*
♠ A K Q 7 3
♡ A K 8 6 2
♢ A K
♣ 4

16
♠ J
♡ J 10 9 2
♢ 10 6 5 3 2
♣ Q 5 2

17
♠ A J 8
♡ K Q
♢ K 10 9 2
♣ 8 7 4 3

18
♠ 10 5
♡ 10 9 8 7 4
♢ 10 6
♣ J 9 8 7

19*
♠ 5
♡ A 9 8 5 4 2
♢ Q 9 2
♣ 10 6 3

20
♠ 5 3
♡ Q J 7 6 2
♢ 6 4 2
♣ A Q 7

21
♠ Q J 6
♡ 10 5 4
♢ K Q J 2
♣ A Q 5

22
♠ 7 6 5
♡ 10 3
♢ A Q 5 4
♣ Q J 10 9

23*
♠ A K 9 8 7 6
♡ J 7
♢ J 3
♣ K J 10

24
♠ 8 7 4 3 2
♡ 9 8
♢ A
♣ A K 10 9 3

Play Hands for WEST (* = dealer)

1
♠ A Q 2
♥ K 9 3
♦ A J 7 2
♣ J 5 3

2
♠ A 3
♥ A K 8 7 6
♦ A 8 4 3 2
♣ K

3
♠ Q 10 9 3
♥ 7 5 4
♦ 9
♣ 10 9 7 5 3

4*
♠ Q J 10 7 4
♥ J 8 6
♦ J 2
♣ A 9 8

5
♠ 10 7
♥ Q 9 8 6 5
♦ A 9
♣ A 6 3 2

6
♠ Q 8 5 3
♥ 7 5
♦ 9 8 4 2
♣ A K Q

7
♠ A 9 7 3
♥ A 8 7 6 5 2
♦ A Q J
♣ - - -

8*
♠ A 7
♥ 7 5
♦ A Q 10 6 2
♣ K J 10 3

9
♠ 10 8 6
♥ K 9 4 2
♦ A J 10 6
♣ K 9

10
♠ 9
♥ K Q 5 4 3
♦ A 5 4 2
♣ Q 7 3

11
♠ J 10 9 8
♥ 2
♦ J 9 8 3 2
♣ K Q 5

12*
♠ K 5 4 3
♥ K 2
♦ 5 3
♣ A Q 7 3 2

13
♠ 7 6
♥ 10 6 4
♦ A 10 5 2
♣ J 7 4 2

14
♠ K 9 8 3
♥ 9
♦ 10 5 3 2
♣ K Q J 7

15
♠ J 9 8 4 2
♥ 10
♦ Q J 10 5
♣ K 10 6

16*
♠ A K 9 8 7 6
♥ A K Q
♦ A K J
♣ 7

17
♠ 9 4 3 2
♥ 9 7 6 5 2
♦ 8 4 3
♣ 5

18
♠ Q 8 4
♥ A Q 3
♦ A K J
♣ Q 10 4 3

19
♠ A Q J 8 7 6
♥ - - -
♦ A K
♣ A K Q 9 8

20*
♠ J 10 7 4 2
♥ 9
♦ J 10 9
♣ K J 10 4

21
♠ 10 9 3 2
♥ A 6
♦ 9 7 5
♣ 10 6 4 2

22
♠ A K Q 9
♥ K 5 4
♦ J 8 7 6
♣ 5 4

23
♠ 4 3 2
♥ Q 9 2
♦ 10 8 7 6
♣ A Q 9

24*
♠ - - -
♥ A K Q 6 5 4
♦ J 9 8 2
♣ Q J 7

RUBBER BRIDGE SCORING TABLE

POINTS TOWARDS GAME UNDER THE LINE :

No-trumps— 10 points plus, per trick . . .	30
Spades or Hearts (major suits) per trick . . .	30
Diamonds or Clubs (minor suits) per trick . . .	20

Final contract doubled and made : Double the above values
Final contract redoubled and made : Above values x 4

BONUS POINTS ABOVE THE LINE :

OVERTRICKS		*Not vulnerable*	*Vulnerable*
For each	Not doubled	Trick value	Trick value
overtrick	Doubled	100	200
	Redoubled	200	400

SLAMS BID AND MADE	*Not vulnerable*	*Vulnerable*
Small slam . . .	500	750
Grand slam . . .	1000	1500

FOR DEFEATING A CONTRACT :

Not doubled, each undertrick : 50 not vulnerable, 100 if vulnerable
Doubled, not vul. : 1st undertrick 100, 2nd and 3rd 200, others 300
Doubled and vulnerable : 1st undertrick 200, all others 300
Redoubled : All undertricks score at twice the doubled rate above

FOR MAKING A DOUBLED CONTRACT :	50
FOR MAKING A REDOUBLED CONTRACT :	100

FOR HONOURS :

Four trump honours in one hand . . .	100
Five trump honours in one hand . . .	150
Four aces in one hand if contract is no-trumps . . .	150

(Either side can score honours which are claimed at the end of play.)

FOR FINISHING THE RUBBER :

For scoring two games to nil . . .	700
For scoring two games to one . . .	500
For one game if the rubber is unfinished . . .	300
For partscore if rubber is unfinished . . .	50

(If scoring game by game : Game 1 : 350, Game 2 : 350, Game 3 : 500.)